THE FLY BY NIGHTS

THE FLY BY NIGHTS

RAF Bomber Command Sorties 1944–45

Donald 'Don' W. Feesey

Pen & Sword
AVIATION

First published in Great Britain in 2007 by
Pen & Sword Aviation
an imprint of
Pen & Sword Books Ltd
47 Church Street
Barnsley
South Yorkshire
S70 2AS

ISBN 1 84415 470 X
978 1 84415 470 8

A CIP catalogue record for this book is
available from the British Library.

Typeset in Palatino by
Phoenix Typesetting, Auldgirth, Dumfriesshire

Printed and bound in England by
Biddles Ltd., King's Lynn

Pen & Sword Books Ltd incorporates the imprints of Pen & Sword Aviation,
Pen & Sword Maritime, Pen & Sword Military, Wharncliffe Local History,
Pen & Sword Select, Pen & Sword Military Classics and Leo Cooper.

For a complete list of Pen & Sword titles please contact
PEN & SWORD BOOKS LIMITED
47 Church Street, Barnsley, South Yorkshire, S70 2AS, England
E-mail: enquiries@pen-and-sword.co.uk
Website: www.pen-and-sword.co.uk

Acknowledgements

My acknowledgements and thanks go firstly to Jim Wright whose excellent publication On Wings of War – (A History of 166 Squadron) was of enormous assistance to me. My thanks also to Anne and David Lee, and to Ron Hales and Peter Turley, the two air gunners in my crew, for their vigilance during our many excursions, and for their continuing friendship and cheerfulness. I must also thank the other members of my crew who are no longer with us – George Lee, "Nobby" Clarke, Ray Forbes and Max Leversha – for their loyalty, trustworthiness and dedicated contributions to our many safe returns.

My wife, Daphne, has my deep love and thanks for her understanding of the hours (years ?) spent compiling this work, and her forbearance on the masses of papers which for so long littered our rooms.

Finally, in view of the headings to some of the chapters in this book, my apologies to all exponents of latin, and my thanks to those having a gsoh.

Don Feesey, 2006

Preface

This book is about the lives of airmen who flew in World War II and, particularly, about the aircrews of Bomber Command as they embarked in complete darkness on their terrifying nightly missions over Germany in 1944 and 1945.

When war was declared in September 1939, the author, Don Feesey, was only sixteen and was studying for a career in The Civil Service. Two years later he volunteered for RAF service as a pilot. Having experienced the German air raids on London in 1940 he felt it his duty to train as a fighter pilot to defend his country. He had no wish to kill German civilians or to destroy their cities by bombing them. The RAF, however, assigned him not to the defensive role he sought, but to an attacking one in Bomber Command.

In all, he made thirty-four successful, long distance sorties over Germany in a four-engined Lancaster bomber. In 1944/45 the aircrews of Bomber Command operated almost entirely on dark nights, usually in dense cloud with no visual navigation to guide them. They were, indeed, the 'fly by nights'.

Few raids were without incident, and in the course of his tour of operations the author lost quite a number of his squadron colleagues, and he saw several aircraft around him blown to pieces or spiralling to their doom.

Here, he describes not only the fears, excitement and tragedies of his crew and others, but also the less well-known months of intensive class-room training, tests and examinations they underwent before qualifying for their wings.

The RAF motto 'Per Ardua Ad Astra' (By Hard Work to the Stars) seemed to the trainee aircrews to be 'Per Ardua Ad Infinitum'! It was quite an achievement just to survive training. Thereafter, survival was largely a matter of luck.

Contents

CONTENTS

CHAPTER ONE

Per Ardua Ad Domesticus

'FLY-BY-NIGHTS' describes those who indulge in despicable vanishing acts known as 'Moonlighting'. This book, however, is about RAF Bomber Command 'fly-by-nights' – the aircrews whose bravery and courage were put to the test in 1944/45, usually when there was no moon at all.

Somewhat reluctantly, I became one of those. I wanted to be a fighter pilot. But it was not to be.

I came into this world four years after the end of the First World War (1914–1918) and, as a child, those wartime years seemed to me to be ancient history. I had a happy childhood both at home and at school, with many friends, but without any interest in politics, foreign affairs or wars. It was not until late in 1938 (when I was 15) that I began to realise that someone called Hitler could possibly involve Britain, and myself, in a war.

Towards the end of August 1939, I went on holiday to Ilfracombe with my parents and my brother. It was glorious weather and wonderfully peaceful. We swam in the sea and sunbathed, but as we lay on the rocks reading our newspapers we found them full of reports of German tanks and infantry threatening Poland. With Britain committed to assisting Poland in the event of enemy attacks, British preparations for war had already begun. Gas masks had been issued to everyone, and civil defence measures put into operation.

Prime Minister Neville Chamberlain had averted war a year earlier when he had met Hitler in Munich in an attempt to negate Germany's policy of *lebensraum* (annexation of neighbouring countries). On his return to London he held up a piece of paper for the waiting newsmen to see, declaring that it bore 'Herr Hitler's signature' for 'Peace In Our Time'. This became known as an act of appeasement.

Germany invaded Poland on 1 September 1939. It was clear that Hitler

1

intended to grab the whole of Europe bit by bit. In 1938 he had taken over Austria, without bloodshed, claiming that he was uniting the German races (known as the *Anschluss*), and then he prepared to take over the Sudetenland (part of Czechoslovakia). To avoid bloodshed, President Haka of Czechoslovakia signed over the whole of his country to the Germans shortly after relinquishing the Sudetenland.

On the invasion of Poland, an ultimatum was sent to Germany from Britain stating that unless an undertaking was received by 11 am on Sunday 3 September for the withdrawal from Poland, a state of war would exist with Britain. By 11 am on that day, radios all over the country were turned on as the nation waited for an announcement from Mr Chamberlain. He announced that no undertaking had been received and so from that moment we were at war with Germany. France declared war a little later the same day and from that time the two countries were jointly 'the Allies'.

I was exactly two months short of my 17th birthday.

At the end of the Prime Minister's announcement we sat silently for a few moments in shock while we all assessed what it would mean to us. Having been issued with gas masks, we had a fear of gas attacks so insulating the house against gas penetration seemed a priority. We would also have to find the safest part of the house to avoid bomb blast during air raids.

But within a few minutes of Mr Chamberlain's speech, the air raid sirens began their terrifying, fluctuating wail. Stomachs tautened through fear. Fleets of German planes could soon be dropping bombs or gas on London. We had decided that our long L-shaped hall would be the safest part of the house and, on hearing the sirens, my mother, in a panic I had never expected of her, rushed up the stairs and threw down a thick double mattress. My brother and I held it over the front door, while our father banged very long nails through it to fix it to the lintel. The air raid warning lasted about 20 minutes, and turned out to be a false alarm due to misidentification of a British aircraft. But it was enough to make the nation realize that a war had begun.

I had left school a year earlier and had just finished a full-time correspondence course in preparation for examinations for the Civil Service. The examinations in those days covered a wide range of subjects and were highly competitive. Intensive study had been my lot for the past twelve months and I was due to take my first exam on 5 September. On 4 September a telegram came saying that all exams had been cancelled until the end of hostilities. If, previously I had no real dislike of Hitler, now I did.

My father was a civil servant and he had to arrange the evacuation of his section from Whitehall to Derbyshire. He went off to Matlock. My brother was in his second year of training at the Royal Aeronautical

College at Chelsea and he travelled there every day from our home in Catford in south-east London. I was left at home with mother and had the task of making the house safe from bombing or gas attacks.

This involved pasting transparent cellophane to the window panes and criss-crossing them with bands of sticky tape to prevent injury from splintering glass. We no longer used the front door – the heavy mattress was hanging behind it – so I sealed this, and a side door, by taping all the edges. This left one remaining exterior door which we used thereafter, and this I taped so that when closed it was fairly well sealed. All window frames were treated similarly. I filled the gaps around skirting boards and between floorboards with newspaper soaked in flour and water paste which dried in a few days and made good seals. Carpets, linoleum and furniture all had to be removed, of course, and replaced, and it took me about six weeks to get it all finished. Fortunately, in that period there were no air raids and there were no gas attacks, but it was essential to be well prepared.

The war at that time had barely disrupted normal life in London. There were occasional siren warnings but there were no raids that I can recall. The main inconvenience was the 'blackout'. All windows had to be covered, there were no street lights and vehicles had to use masked head-lights. There was a heavy demand for torch batteries.

One by one my older friends were being called up and I knew that my turn would be coming soon. I had no wish to go to war. So far as I was concerned, fighting was no way to settle a dispute. Having an older and stronger brother I had learned that lesson long ago!

I felt it morally wrong to kill young Germans who, I assumed, were as innocent and indifferent to war as myself. Tyrants such as Hitler needed to be apprehended, tried and imprisoned or hanged but not by involving whole nations in war. To conscript young innocent boys to be killed for the ideals of unstable, power-mad dictators disgusted me.

My closest school chum was a little older and joined the RAF to train as a fighter pilot, as did another close friend who lived two doors away. In 1940, both were shot down and killed. To lose them within a few weeks of each other was a shattering blow and their deaths caused me to recon-sider my attitude to war. The Germans could not be allowed to overrun one country after another, and our country had to be defended. As fighter pilots were primarily defenders, I reasoned that my beliefs would not be betrayed if I joined the RAF with that aim. Attacking German cities and killing innocent civilians had no appeal, but defending my own country was a different matter.

By this time, I had entered the Civil Service as a temporary clerk. I served for a month or two as a 'dogsbody' in an employment exchange, after which my abilities were reassessed and I was rewarded with a transfer to H.M. Treasury.

On 10 July 1940 the Battle of Britain began, leading to the blitz on London. The fighter pilots were fully engaged with their defensive activities. On the ground, life consisted of making one's way to work by whatever routes were available through the glass-strewn, cratered streets, and back in the evening – to go straight down into the air raid shelter where my mother had prepared some food. We stayed there all night while the battle raged above.

CHAPTER TWO

Bellum Ova
Britannicus

In the Spring of 1940, Germany's strategic attacks on Norway, Denmark and Holland had led to the conquering of these countries. There followed the destruction of the northern part of the French Maginot Line (defence posts connected by underground tunnels) forcing the Allied troops to be evacuated at Dunkirk with the aid of the flotilla of 'little ships'. The French surrendered and the war against Britain began in earnest.

The German offensive began by concentrating on the many airfields in the south-east where most of the British fighter squadrons were based. They also attacked the southern ports and the Thames estuary. Initially these were daylight raids but soon attacks were launched by day and by night.

The bombers were careful not to attack London for fear of reprisals on Berlin, which at that time had not been affected by the war and was still lit up at night. However, towards the end of August 1940 the Islington/Stepney area of London was bombed – possibly by mistake. The RAF mounted the reprisal raids expected of them and the German blitz on London began.

The heaviest bombing occurred between the 7 and 15 September with sporadic attacks until 5 October. Hitler had been expecting to be able to force Britain to surrender by 15 September, but the RAF fighters and ground defences thwarted him. Nevertheless, the damage and casualties, particularly in London Docks area, were enormous, and life in the whole of London was badly dislocated.

The German bombers were mainly Junkers 87s and 88s, Heinkel 111s and Dornier 17s and 217s. The Dorniers were known as 'flying pencils' because of their long slender fuselage and they had a distinctive throbbing note to their engines. The Ju 87, or 'Stuka', was a dive bomber. It had a fixed undercarriage to which were attached 'Jericho' sirens which emitted a piercing shriek designed to instil fear in people below. The defences of barrage balloons, anti-aircraft guns and searchlights provided reassurance, although the noise of the guns, the falling shrapnel, the 'Jericho' sirens and, the exploding bombs after they had whistled down, leading to severe fire damage, were much to contend with.

By this time, my father had been evacuated not to Matlock but to Reading. The strain of the air raids and being alone all day had unnerved my mother. She decided to join my father, and my brother and I went with her to Reading. My brother had become a civilian aircraft engineer and was exempt from military service. I travelled to and from my Treasury job in London until the end of the year when I was able to transfer to the Ministry of Health Regional Office in Reading.

Being then eighteen, I volunteered for RAF service as aircrew. I went before an assessment panel of three elderly officers (one from each Service) who were not impressed with my earlier pacifist views, and I was rejected. However, by this time I was convinced that Europe had to be saved from tyranny and our own country had to be defended. I strongly wanted to do my bit and felt that I could best do so in the Air Force. I was already serving in the ATC (Air Training Corps) and with my Commanding Officer's testimonial I went before another Board and was accepted with a recommendation for pilot training. I expected to start almost at once, but it transpired that there was a surfeit of trainee pilots at the time and I was deferred until June 1942.

There was a lull in British military action and Hitler must have felt so sure of winning that he embarked on an invasion of Russia in June 1941. Here, in Britain we did not regard Russia as friendly, yet, strangely as it might seem, Communist Russia now became one of the Allies.

With German action against Britain reduced, I welcomed the opportunity to seek some pleasure during my period of deferment. Reading had not experienced any of the horrors suffered by London, and there were numerous leisure activities available.

The Ministry offices were dispersed over several closely sited requisitioned houses and every night and all over weekends staff members undertook firewatching duties in case of attacks. As I was one of the youngest members of staff, with no family commitments, I not only took my turn, but also acted as a reserve if needed. Sometimes, I was on duty twice a week. To overcome boredom I kept my gramophone at the office and listened to my records. I was alone one weekend when a more senior member of staff came back to do some work and heard me singing away in accompaniment to a Nelson Eddy record in my upstairs room. He came up and told me he was organising a concert party for the YWCA (Young Women's Christian Association) and needed some male singers. I went along for a rehearsal and found he had also invited a young girl from one of the other office houses. Her name was Daphne Orchard and we worked together on several of the sketches. At the end of the rehearsal, I found that she lived quite close to my home. She was the only one going my way so we walked home together in the blackout – and continued to do so after subsequent rehearsals.

The concert party was great fun and Daphne and I became good friends. When a vacancy occurred in her firewatching squad, I joined it and we used to sit up in our attic duty room with the gramophone listening to the records into the early morning hours. Our 'romance' as it was known in the office was quite a talking point and watched with interest. Some said that it was just 'Puppy Love'. How wrong they were! We went on to get married – deferred because of the war – and we have enjoyed 60 years of very happy marriage.

This period of my life was a busy, as well as an enjoyable, time. At last I was able to have a social life. Concert Party rehearsals and ATC training were just part of it. I played for the Ministry table-tennis and darts teams and, being a keen footballer, I trained one evening a week with the Reading Football Club. In the summer, there was cricket and tennis, and, occasionally I would go to musical concerts where I acquired an understanding of Haydn and Mozart string quartets. I went to these alone as Daphne's ears were not attuned to chamber music! Foolishly, I took her one evening to hear Bach's Mass in B Minor which was a mistake. The fact that she continued seeing me was proof that it was not just 'Puppy Love'!

Sadly the time came for me to go into the Air Force. We both knew that I might never come back. But like so many others in wartime we could only hope that luck would be on our side. So as we parted, the song 'I'll See You Again' helped us to put our faith in our futures.

CHAPTER THREE

Per Ardua Ad-Justera

In July 1942 I was called up to the Aircrew Receiving Centre (ACRC) at Lords cricket ground near St John's Wood. Here we were kitted out and became acquainted with medicals, vaccinations, marching drills and guard duties.

All aircrew trainees were volunteers. Other airmen were conscripted and known as 'draftees' – not inferring that they were in any way 'windy'! As trainee aircrew we wore white flashes in our caps and had the letters 'VR' (Volunteer Reserve) on each shoulder beneath the RAF eagle emblem.

At the end of our first week we were looking forward to a weekend leave but, at the last moment we were marched to Regents Park to take part in a film with Vera Lynn entertaining the troops. We were required to wave and cheer enthusiastically, which was hard to do, having been denied our leave. I found it especially galling, being none too keen on Vera Lynn's squeaky sort of voice. She was very young and I enjoyed her singing much more when she had matured.

The next weekend, we were definitely promised leave and after two, not very enjoyable, weeks, the anticipation was heavenly. I planned to go home to Reading but early on the Saturday morning word came through that there was a smallpox outbreak there, so, for me, leave was cancelled. Surprisingly, they let me out to phone my parents, who let Daphne know.

Miserably, I watched the others depart. Then, at midday, I was summoned to the Orderly Room and told that the smallpox report had been found incorrect and I could start my leave. I made my way to Swiss Cottage underground station and changed at Baker Street. As I walked along the platform, who should I see coming towards me but Daphne! She had decided that if I couldn't get to her she would come to me. Luckily she had got on to the wrong platform or we would have missed each other. Strangely, we met by chance on several other occasions during the war. It was evidently meant to be.

It goes without saying that we had a magnificent weekend together and it was with reluctance that I made my way back to my unit by midnight on Sunday.

For many of us, the RAF was something new and some aspects of Service discipline were not easy to accept. The discipline was intended to toughen us up and to break our spirits by getting us accustomed to being humiliated and punished at the whim of any sadistically minded officer or NCO for failing to comply with some nonsensical regulation. Such regulations were known as 'bullshit', a term which covered also the unnecessary polishing of boots or buttons and the sprucing up of accommodation, uniforms or equipment. Rumours or unfounded information were 'a load of bull'.

We were accommodated in fairly new blocks of flats overlooking Regents Park. I was in one called Viceroy Court. The rooms had been stripped and contained only iron bedsteads on bare wooden floors. All doors and fittings had been removed but there were still washbasins, baths and WCs. Inspections were made at any time of day to check that floorboards had been swept and scrubbed, toilets and baths cleaned, and bedding laid out in exactly the pattern shown to us on arrival. Shiny boots and buttons were being checked continually and our RAF pay of two shillings a day (ten new pence) was eaten into by purchases of Cherry Blossom and Silvo.

We were told that at the end of week two, the Flight with the shiniest boots would be rewarded with a forty-eight hour pass, so that was an incentive. The boots issued to me were made of a dull, oily leather giving the appearance of having been treated with dubbin – a waterproofing grease which I used on my football boots. After three days, I had used up half a tin of black boot polish and the boots still looked dull. We were shown how to mix the polish with our spittle (spit and polish) and while other chaps got their boots to shine, my spittle seemed to be made up of the wrong chemical formula.

As the whole Flight would suffer if one pair of boots was unacceptable, I worried that the other lads would take it out of me for letting them down. The other fellows in my room knew about it and tried to bring up a shine but all to no avail. They suggested that I should ask the Flight NCO to let me change the boots, but all he said was 'Keep at it lad and they'll shine'. We decided that the rest of the Flight in the other rooms needed to be told about it and several of them had a go at polishing and realised there was a problem. We tried rubbing the leather with a bone and with an ivory shoehorn but the greasy tops were unchanged. I managed to get out one night to phone my father (an old soldier) for advice and he sent me some vinegar to neutralise the oil. It made no difference. I went again to the Corporal and at last he realised that those boots were never going to shine and that it would reflect badly on him if his Flight lost the contest. He gave me a note to take to the clothing store and I was able to pick out a slightly worn pair of boots with a good shine on them. The inspection took place the following day, and our Flight got the leave. But it had been an acutely distressing start to my air force career.

My mother had sent me the vinegar in a food parcel, but we were not allowed to have any personal property on display and there were no cupboards or places where I could hide it. My room mates and I shared most of the food and what was left I tried to stuff into my kitbag. In doing so, I tore off the covering flap and for the first time in my life I had to try my hand at sewing. (Airmen were issued with a 'hussif' [or 'housewife'] of scissors, needle and thread.) Remarkably that kitbag flap stayed put right through the war!

Before I close this chapter, I must refer once more to the 'bull' we encountered. As it was summertime, our greatcoats and uniform jackets had to be correctly folded and laid out on our beds all day for inspection, while we paraded and drilled in our shirtsleeves. However, these shirtsleeves were not allowed to be rolled up outwards in the usual way, but INWARDS AND TO THE REGULATION HEIGHT.

Adjusting to the idiosyncrasies of Service life was not easy – hence the title to the chapter!

CHAPTER FOUR

Tempus Grandioso

After nineteen days at ACRC we were posted to an ACD (Air Crew Disposal) wing at Brighton, which turned out to be the requisitioned Grand Hotel on the seafront. This being the hotel in which the IRA (Irish Republican Army) detonated a bomb some 50 years later when Prime Minister Mrs Thatcher and others were staying there for a Conservative Party conference. After my stay there in 1942 I rarely went near it but, quite by chance, I had to go past it three times during the afternoon just prior to the explosion.

At the Grand, we had to do everything 'at the double' including running up and down the stairs – and I was on the seventh floor!

We also had to keep a gleaming polish on the floorboards of our rooms, plus, to satisfy our sadistic masters, apply black boot polish to the WHITE stone thresholds in every doorway. The inspecting NCO would frequently wipe his boots across these and have them done again.

To think that we were going to be risking our lives for people like him. He was, of course, not one of us, but a 'regular' (yes, a regular . . . !) – the sort who gained pleasure by tormenting those in his power. Let's be clear about this. He was not a 'one off'; we came across many more like him as we proceeded with our training (and after too). We were not only at war with Germany; we had to contend with a sort of 'class' war as well. And training extended over many months; in fact it was over two years before I began my operational flying.

Having carefully rolled up our shirtsleeves inwards to conform with what we believed to be RAF procedure, within an hour we were bellowed at and told to roll them up outwards. Our navy coloured canvas PT (physical training) slippers had to be polished with black boot polish. Hair had to be really short, and extra drills and repeat haircuts were commonplace. It was no wonder that we regarded regular NCOs with contempt.

Doors to the bedrooms were nailed open and the windows had to be kept open to allow the gales off the sea to sweep through. I and seven others were in an attic room facing north at the back of the hotel, with small windows, set high up. Consequently, the room was always dark

11

and we were not allowed lamp bulbs. Nevertheless, we still had to put up blackout material each night.

The poorly lit room was actually an advantage. It prevented the inspecting officer or NCO from seeing any small bits of blanket fluff which we might have overlooked when sweeping. At any rate we always seemed to get away with ours, whereas the lads in the rooms in the front of the building, with large windows overlooking the sea, and with good light, often had to clean their floors again, and were given extra drills or guard duties.

This rankled with them, and late one night the lads from across the passage stormed into our room and began tipping people out of bed and having bolster fights. The fracas heightened and they got hold of the fire buckets and threw water and sand over our floor. With no lights it was impossible to see what state the floor was in, but we were sliding about in our bare feet on the wet, gritty surface. We drove the enemy out, but with the doors nailed back it was simple for them to return later to give us another 'going over'. We saw them off for a second time and, while some of the chaps tried to clear up a bit, I barricaded the doorway by tying strings across it at different heights. When the raiders returned for a third time, the first one nearly strangled himself and it was easy for us to repulse them. Once they had settled down in their own room we refilled the buckets with water and laid them outside their doorway so that they would fall over them in the darkness should they make another foray. But they had had enough. Despite our disturbed night, we had to get up early to make the place clean for inspection. Somehow we managed to get by.

The following night I was in charge of the Defence Patrol and in the early hours of the morning the sirens sounded. That night there had been a dance downstairs and a flight on the landing below ours had attended it and some were drunk. It was my job to get them down to assembly points for a roll call. Some were in bed 'out to the world', some were being sick and some fighting. With help from my squad we were able to get most of them to the safe areas but I had to report to the Duty Officer that others were still upstairs in no state to move. It had been a comic sight seeing semi-clad figures running along corridors and down the stairs – in vests or pyjama tops, but wearing tin hats! I pointed out to the officer that finding everyone was pretty well impossible in pitch darkness. The next day, blue lamp bulbs were fitted on all landings and in the dormitories!

As it happened there was no air raid that night, but on 27 July bombs dropped not far away, and on 8 August in daylight, three low flying Messerschmitt 109s flew past the hotel, about 100 yards from our windows.

Despite all the 'bull' we did actually spend some time on training, with classroom courses on Morse code signalling, arithmetic, aircraft recognition and anti-gas measures, with exams at the end of our stay. Only two chaps failed and were made to stay behind for further training. The rest of us were classified 'Grade A' (which was the term used to describe the best quality pre-war milk!).

We then expected to be posted to an ITW (Initial Training Wing), as had been promised. But, as you will find in the next chapter, we were moved on, not knowing anything about our destination. Moreover, we had been promised seven days leave for having kept our room clean. It was a load of 'bull'!

CHAPTER FIVE

Per Ardua Labore, Aqua et Dis-con-tent

O n Saturday 15 August 1942, we were woken at 5.30 am, given breakfast, and then marched to Brighton Station where we boarded the 8 am train for Victoria. We had no idea where we were going. From Victoria, we were taken in coaches to Addison Road station (later Olympia). There we were given the day's rations – a roll spread with butter and jam, and a piece of cake. We boarded a train still with no knowledge of our destination. At 4.30 pm the train stopped; we were told to get off and we found we were on the platform of Ludlow station in Shropshire.

In full kit we marched off in blazing sunshine up and down hill until we came to some large fields a short way from the town. We went through a gateway manned by an RAF guard and found ourselves in a massive tented camp. This was our destination.

We were taken to a large marquee where we were allowed to take off our heavy kit and greatcoats. A sergeant informed us that we would be staying for about three weeks helping with the construction of the camp. But first we were to be given a meal and taken to the tents in which we would live. Our meagre train rations had been eaten long before, so we were hot, thirsty and hungry. We marched to a mess tent, past an outside row of evil smelling black ranges and we feared the worst. In fact we had a superb meal of sausage, egg and chips, mugs of tea, bread and butter and jam, all prepared by trained airmen cooks and aircrew cadets like ourselves who were on kitchen fatigues.

After we had eaten we were taken to a field about a quarter of a mile away, where there were rows of bell tents. We were assigned to the tents without any choice of our companions. A water standpipe had been erected about fifty yards from the tents, and a bench had been built, on which stood metal bowls where we washed and shaved in the open air, even though the bench was under a canvas tarpaulin supported by iron stanchions. Latrines were some way off and were serviced by whichever of us were detailed for that duty.

Each morning before going off to our duties, we were required to lay all our kit and bedding outside the front of the tent (in the prescribed fashion of course), leaving one cadet in charge of about a dozen tents. If it rained, he had to pack everything up and put it all back in the tents, after letting down the lower storm flaps and slackening the guy ropes. Naturally, this all took a great deal of time, and, understandably, this cadet always took care of his own kit and own tent first. The rest got pretty wet!

We were issued with coupons for cigarettes and sweets but, as our kit was normally laid out in the hot sun, chocolate bars or sweets became a gooey mess.

From time to time we were given training in signalling, maths, navigation, aircraft recognition and anti-gas drill, but these activities came secondary to duties for the running of the camp, including 'construction'.

A roadway was being built across the fields, and lorries brought large white, chalky stones which had to be broken up and stamped into the ground, and rolled. Our boots were soon covered in white dust, and our evenings were spent in cleaning up. We were paraded and inspected in the mornings and assigned to our duties for the day. Despite the un-expected hard work, good humour prevailed and one morning a 'wag' called out, 'C'mon lads, its either cookhouse fatigues or construction, so take your pick!'

One day, when I went down with the construction party, a Flight Sergeant came over and asked if anyone had experience of lettering or poster work. I volunteered and he told me that he was putting on an RAF concert in the town hall and needed someone to draw up about a dozen posters. He took me off to one of the Admin tents and rooted about looking for suitable paper and colours. He found none so he left me to continue searching while he went off on his bike to seek some in the town. He was away most of the day, which suited me. Eventually, I spotted him coming towards me pushing his smashed-up bicycle and with a bandaged hand and chin. He had had an accident and been to Sick Quarters to get patched up. He wasn't very happy as he had found no paint or colours, and only a few sheets of large paper.

The next day he asked me to ride into Ludlow to see what I could find and also to visit a café where I was to ask one of the waitresses he knew of to sing in the concert. She readily agreed and I spent the rest of the day combing the shops for the materials. I found none, but on return to the camp, I explored some of the other Admin tents and found some water-proof colouring inks and paper – which somehow went 'missing'.

So that was two days when I had avoided being on 'construction'. That had not been my intention when I had volunteered; but I now made sure that those twelve posters were not completed too quickly!

Before I had finished, the Flight Sergeant popped in one day to say that Air Vice Marshal Critchley was on his way to inspect the camp and it wouldn't do for him to find me making posters. I had to return to the construction gang. It was pouring with rain so we wore our ground-sheets. Even so, we were soaking wet. The rain was so heavy that it was decided that the AVM should not see us working in such conditions or let him see how bedraggled we were in our wet clothes. We were bundled into a marquee and kept out of sight until he had gone. The rain continued and I went back to my posters. When I got back to my tent after tea, I found my bedding and kit still outside in the rain. Everybody else's had been taken in. Some of the chaps were inside and I asked why they hadn't taken my stuff in. Nobody spoke, and I began to move my sodden bedding into the tent. I had been sent to Coventry, but not realising quite why. Apart from one friend who slept next to me, the others were from the group that had raided our dormitory at the Grand. They were not a nice bunch. My pal came out and helped me with my kit. 'It's their way of punishing you for evading construction work' he explained. Such deliberate spite would never have occurred to me. I had not been brought up that way, and, in any case, I had volunteered merely to be of help and not with any intention to avoid 'construction'.

I learnt later that I was also being ostracized for helping the permanent staff. That, in itself was a crime in their eyes and contravened their code. Instilled in their natures was later what I learnt to call 'north-country trade unionism'. Workers do not help management! Their code also embraced nastiness to anyone more able than themselves. I qualified in all ways!

Having displayed their jealously at the Grand because they had been punished more often than us for the state of their room, they had now gratified themselves by allowing my kit and bedding to be saturated by the rain. And, I found it was not just by the rain. My water bottle had been uncorked and tipped into the top of my kitbag.

Being 'soft' southerners, the next day my mate and I moved into another tent.

The concert in the town hall was very good, especially the contribution by a Corporal Terry O'Farrell, who told jokes and had a superb tenor voice. The next day, when we were clearing up the hall, he gave us some very professional renderings of 'Questa o Quella' and 'La Donna e Mobile' from Rigoletto.

While in the town I took the opportunity of looking for accommodation for my girl friend, Daphne, who was about to join the WAAF (Women's Auxiliary Air Force) and, as we had been apart for some time, she had decided to come to Ludlow. However, The Feathers and The Bull were out of bounds to aircrew cadets. I booked her in at The Compasses. With three other lads who had been helping to clear up the hall, we found a house with a large walled garden and gate marked 'Teas'. We went in and were met by a pleasant middle-aged lady who served us each – a boiled egg, four sandwiches, four slices of bread and butter and raspberry jam, two cakes and tea (from a pot and with cups!) with plenty of milk and sugar. With war-time rationing we had seen nothing like this for years (and certainly not since joining up!). I took Daphne there on the Sunday and we were served the same set tea as before – except that we each had two boiled eggs. The lady explained that she kept hens. She found us a secluded place in the garden and then said that as it looked like rain, we could go into the summer house and stay as long as we liked. It did rain and we stayed all the evening until it was time for me to escort Daphne back to her hotel and wish her goodnight and goodbye. Our lovely weekend was over and I made my way, desolately, back to my inferior accommodation.

We still talk of the kindness shown to us that day for it meant much to us. We were very much in love and we wrote to each other nearly every day. The letters were full of news as well as endearments, and we have kept them. They have been invaluable in helping me to write this book.

A few days before I was due to be posted to an ITW (Initial Training Wing), I developed swollen legs, which became so painful that I could barely walk. It was probably due to the wet conditions. I was admitted to Sick Quarters. This was a luxurious brick building and deliciously warm. I was given a hot bath, clean, warm (and dry) pyjamas, and put into a real bed with a mattress and sheets! The blankets were dry too. I wondered why I had not thought of going sick, earlier!

My flight had been told that we were to be posted to the ITW at Torquay, and that was the one I had particularly hoped for. Consequently, after a few days, I declared myself fit, even though my legs were still not right. I reported back to my corporal, but my name had already been removed from the list and so all my friends went without me.

Cadets who missed their postings were assigned to an assortment of chores for the next three weeks, until the next batch of postings were prepared. Some of these assignments were somewhat unsavoury. There were only a few of us left behind, so it was odds on us being put on to the dirtiest jobs. For once, fortune was on my side. I met up with a fellow who was rather older than the others, and who had been left over from an even earlier intake than ours, as he was awaiting a compassionate posting to the ITW at Cambridge, which was where he lived. As he was being held at Ludlow for some time, the CO had asked him to construct a large, scale model of the town and the camp. This was a big job and he got the CO's permission to have me as his assistant. This got us off camp duties and we had a free pass to go 'off limits' into the town and the surrounding countryside to sketch and make models of the buildings, woods etc. We had a massive plywood sheet on which we constructed models out of putty, wood, plaster and sand, and painted the buildings, bridges, river, trees and fields in the appropriate colours. It was a really fascinating pastime, and the freedom we had been given was exquisite. Of course, we never finished.

At the end of the three weeks, I was posted to no 9 ITW at Stratford-on-Avon and, by that time, my colleague, Bill Bailey, no longer needed a Cambridge posting so he came too.

CHAPTER SIX

Per '(B) Ardua' Domicilum et Rank Injustice

At Stratford-on-Avon, Shakespeare's birthplace, we were assigned to the requisitioned Avonside Hotel. It was a very old building (now demolished and rebuilt) situated a little way out of the town, near the parish church, at the end of a cul-de-sac. The grounds ran down to the River Avon, and the hotel was mainly used by officers on the Admin staff. A long, rather dilapidated hut in the grounds housed some cadets from an earlier intake, and we were put into a fairly modern house called Avonfield on the opposite side of the road.

Our lectures and lessons were held in more requisitioned hotels in the centre of the town, where other flights were billeted. We were marched between the hotels at the fast rate of 120 paces to the minute, and as our flight was billeted further out than the others we did rather more marching. Perhaps, because of this, we managed to win the drill competition. We even went on to give exhibitions of continuity drill – movements from memory, without commands, which we learnt from two large sheets of paper.

We had a Welsh corporal with a very high voice and when we first began our drilling it took us a while to understand his exaggerated commands which sounded like 'ST-H-ANDAHT-HEISS' and 'HABBOW-CHURR'. During our first parade he sneezed and a few of us 'about turned'!

Here, at last, we started real training for aircrew duties. The course included RAF law, hygiene, maths, Morse signalling by wireless and by Aldiss Lamp, meteorology, elementary navigation, aircraft recognition, armaments and shooting practice at moving targets (clay pigeons). There was plenty of voluntary study to be done in the evenings, but we were free to go into the town. As a rule, we were off duty at weekends but we could not obtain passes to travel beyond the town.

Daphne was still waiting to go into the WAAF and as I could not get to see her, I sought and found for her some accommodation in a private house on the Evesham Road for a weekend. I was able to show her Shakespeare's birthplace, Anne Hathaway's cottage and the fine churches and buildings in the town. We met up with Bill Bailey and with his usual exuberance he vaulted over a low wall and picked her a red rose from one of the Corporation flower beds. That was Bill Bailey.

Shortly afterwards, Daphne was called up and had to report to Gloucester. In her first letter to me she wrote of the problems of mastering front and back collar studs and how to do up a tie! In a few days she was moved on to Morecambe where she was lucky to be billeted with a wonderful landlady who gave her good food and plenty of it. She probably needed it as the girls underwent intensive drilling, much of it in gas masks and gas capes.

In her next letter, she told me she had been to a dance. She should have had a pass and she wrote – 'I borrowed one off another girl and altered it. Is this allowed?'

On 14 November 1942 she was posted to the RAF Record Office at Gloucester, and remained there for the rest of the war, as a Clerk GD (General Duties). She enjoyed herself there as Gloucester was basically unaffected by the war. She went to cinemas, concerts, dances and Service clubs and canteens so there were many social activities available, plus American Service personnel who saw that the girls had a good time.

Back at Stratford, our instruction was extended to include shooting on the rifle range and bayonet practice. The latter had little appeal, until I learnt to imagine the stuffed dummy to be our CO, who, in true moronic RAF fashion, had punished the whole flight because four of the lads had got drunk and not returned until late at night.

A number of us were down with colds at this time. We had had a lot of rain and some early snow, and, to make way for a new intake, we had been moved from the comfort of Avonfield House to the dilapidated hut in the hotel grounds. It had a stone floor, the roof leaked, and we were not the only occupants. Overnight, our socks on the racks above our beds were attacked by mice. Darning them was a regular activity.

With all the snow and sleet it was difficult to keep our boots clean when we were marched between the different hotels. One evening my mate, Bill, had to go to an Admin section in another hotel to arrange for a pass. The SP (Station Policeman) on duty clearly wanted someone to have a go at. He looked Bill up and down and demanded 'When did you last clean your boots?' 'This morning' replied Bill. The SP sarcastically said, 'That's funny, so did I, and my boots are much shinier than yours'. Bill, being a cheeky, effervescent character was never stuck for a riposte. 'There's nothing funny about that', he answered. 'I've been marching about all day in mucky streets while you've been lolling around in this nice warm office!' Anyone else would have been put on a charge for such insolence, but Bill could get away with such things. That was Bill Bailey.

At the end of the course, we took our exams and were selected for continued training as pilots, navigators, bomb-aimers, wireless operators or gunners. Over the ten examinations I had an average mark of 85 per cent which I thought to be pretty good, only to find I was only twelfth out of twenty-nine on the course. Most of us were selected for pilot training.

With the relief at finishing the course, we went back to our cold hut in an exuberant mood, and we knew that at last we were going to get some leave. But there were still guard duties and fire picket duties to be done by some that night. The fire picket was made up of four cadets. I was sitting on my bed just inside the hut doorway when the corporal in charge burst in, shouting 'I've only got three fire pickets – where's the fourth?' Without a thought, I called out 'In Scotland of course!' There was a roar of laughter and the corporal stood looking perplexed before departing, probably believing that the missing 'bod' had gone up north.

Bill Bailey was so delighted with his selection for pilot that he acquired another red rose for me to send to Daphne with the good news. We were given nine days leave from Friday 11 December and Daphne managed to get leave until the 16th too. It was my first leave for four months and I felt quite tired after so much concentrated studying and exams. Consequently, I was somewhat quiet and withdrawn and as Daphne did not get all the attention she was hoping for, she was a bit put out.

On my return to Stratford, we found we had been moved to another hotel – the Washington Irving – where we were put into attic rooms which were exceedingly cold. We no longer belonged to our old 'A Flight', but became 'X Flight'. Until we could be posted we were to be held doing whatever odd jobs – unpleasant ones as a rule – that could be found for us.

There followed some rank injustice. Since joining up, we had been Aircraftsmen Second Class (AC2s). On completing an ITW course it was the practice for the cadets to become Leading Aircraftsmen (LACs) and to wear propeller symbols on the arms of their uniforms. Suddenly an order came out that nobody would be allowed to wear badges of rank, so there would be no 'props' and we would all be known merely as cadets. Now, training on our course we had a Warrant Officer, a sergeant, a corporal and an existing LAC who had remustered to aircrew trainees, but who had existing substantive ranks. They were required to take down their badges of rank. It was socialism gone made! Everyone had to be equal! There was not exactly a mutiny, but we all kicked up a hell of a rumpus and eventually the stupidity of the order was realized and it was rescinded.

CHAPTER SEVEN

Ashes to Ashes, Dust to Dust

Our upgrading did not excuse us from whatever chores had to be done. A particularly nasty one came my way early in January 1943. Six of us were ordered to the armoury, where we were issued with dirty overalls and a shovel each. A corporal then led us in single file to the Avonside Hotel (our former home). Had a German spy been watching, he would never have guessed that the six scruffy figures in mucky overalls carrying shovels were actually pilots under training.

We were all in a happy mood and instead of being marched, we strolled slowly along the secluded cul-de-sac leading to the hotel. One of the lads called out that we looked like the dwarfs from Snow White. And with that we went on our way singing 'Heigh Ho! Heigh Ho! It's off to work we go'.

Our high spirits vanished once we found out what we had to do. We were given metal dustbins and told to take them into the cellar, where we would find clinker and ashes which had been cleared from the hotel fireplaces. We were to fill the bins and take them across the road and tip them onto the drive of Avonfield House. We descended into the cellar and found the lower steps and floor covered with a firm layer of ashes about two feet deep. They were solid enough for us to walk on them and must have accumulated over many years. We began to fill our dustbins but, within a few seconds the air in the confined space was filled with choking grey dust. With no face masks, we were all gasping and choking. We made our way outside and complained to the corporal, but he told us the job had to be done and we should tie handkerchiefs over our faces.

We waited for the dust to settle and then planned how to proceed. We decided that only two at a time should go into the cellar and fill just one bin. They would then carry the bin across the road and empty it while the next pair went down into the cellar. It slowed our progress but it kept the dust down to a reasonable level. There were stoppages while we coughed and spluttered and we did not empty the cellar until well into the afternoon. By that time, we were covered in dust from head to foot and our mouths and noses were lined with the stuff. We had had no lunch, but, knowing the hotel layout, we knew where we could find water to swill out our mouths. The corporal had vanished.

Having completed the task, we expected to be told to spread the ashes over the driveway of Avonfield. Instead, a lorry arrived with the corporal and we were instructed to fill the dustbins once again and to empty them into the back of the lorry. A pity someone had not thought of providing the lorry earlier; it would have saved a lot of work! Having filled the lorry, we were told to climb up and sit on top of the ashes, with our shovels, and we were driven to the narrow rutted track which led to the rifle range. Every time the lorry jolted over a rut or a hole, the dust swirled up around our faces. There had been rain and snow for several days and the track was muddy and waterlogged. The potholes were not visible. Occasionally the lorry wheels sank and we had to jump down and shovel ashes round them in order to get moving. Finally, we came to a part of the track which was completely submerged. It was only then that we were told what the ashes were for. We had to shovel them out into the pool ahead of us. Of course the lorry was stuck facing the wrong way for us to shovel ashes straight down off the back of it! It became clear why the RAF motto began 'PER ARDUA . . .'!

When the lorry was emptied, it was reversed up the track with us trudging behind through the mud and wet ashes. We were driven back to the Washington Irving Hotel – back entrance so as not to be seen by the public – and fortunately there was hot water where we could clean up and go for our first meal since breakfast.

A few of the fellows tended to get a bit despondent by the way we were being treated, but in the main, we recognised that there were certain jobs which had to be done, and if, for some reason, our flying training could not proceed, then it fell to us to have to do them. But it was not what we had volunteered for. To maintain spirits, I penned a poem and pinned it to our door:-

'X Flight – The Sweepers'
We're the Flight, that does the chores
Scrubs the tables, sweeps the floors.
We do all odd jobs there are.
So they've sacked the Squadron 'char'.
Clean the windows, polish brass.
Trim the edges of the grass.
Fill all potholes up with tar,
Even clean the 'Old Man's' car.
Sweep the pavements clear of snow,

Till the gutters overflow.
Remove the muck that blocks the drains,
Getting filthy for our pains.
Clean the bathrooms and latrines.
Help the cook to wash the greens.
Wash the cabbage, peel the spuds,
Wash up crocks – but don't use suds!
Fill the boilers up with coke,
Fill the kitchen full of smoke.
Rummage through the garbage heap
For things the sergeant wants to keep.
Thus as every day goes by,
We wonder when we'll learn to fly.
But when we can, we'll have a try
At sweeping Jerry from the sky!

Now that Daphne was also in the Forces we were uncertain as to how often we would be able to meet. At this time we managed to fit in two short meetings. We looked forward to these snatched hours together, but travelling in those times was exhausting and fraught with anxieties. Trains or buses were suddenly cancelled or delayed, and, for trainees at any rate, there were punishments for reporting back late. On one Sunday I left Reading at 4.30 in the afternoon and eventually reached Birmingham at 3.30 the next morning. The next train to Stratford was the 6.30 am that got me back to my unit just before the expiry of my pass at 8.00 am.

I found that a new intake had arrived from the outdoor camp at Ludlow. They told us that their kits laid outside their tents in the daytime were regularly covered with snow or ice, and that ice formed on their blankets, overnight within the tents. Because of this, they had been held there for only five days and the camp had been closed. (Clearly, some Admin Officer had gone soft!)

This unexpected influx of cadets resulted in X Flight becoming superfluous so far as odd jobs were concerned. Other ideas were thought up to keep us occupied. For a start, we were taken to a nearby aircraft factory to see how Mosquito aeroplanes were built. This was the closest we had been to an aeroplane in the six months of our service.

On another occasion, we were ordered to assemble without any food, sweets or money, and were driven some distance in a covered lorry. We were dropped off in pairs and had to pretend we had baled out of an aircraft in enemy territory, and, without speaking to anyone or asking directions, find our way back to the hotel. I had done some walking in the area some weeks earlier and I had a pretty good idea in which direction to go. Bill Bailey and I were among the first back – but then I had a small compass in my pocket! Some lads were not back until late at night.

Perhaps they thought they had to do the thing properly and travel only in darkness! Or, maybe, they did have some cash with them and found a pub on the way. Surprisingly, nobody went AWOL (absent without leave).

We finally went to an armaments works in a former car factory in Birmingham where we were given an excellent meal and a warm welcome by the young girl munitions-workers. They probably thought we were glamorous heroic airmen. They had not seen us the day before, emptying the pig bins outside the cookhouses and washing out the swill containers. There was no doubt that they were doing far more for the war effort than we were being permitted to do.

CHAPTER EIGHT

A Tiger in the Meadow

On 22 January 1943, I and a few of my colleagues were posted to No. 28 EFTS (Elementary Flying Training School) on the municipal airport about six miles north of Wolverhampton. We were immediately allocated to our instructors and began dual-control flying in Tiger Moths.

On the ground, we familiarized ourselves with the aircraft and the controls – how the control column operated the ailerons on the wings to cause the machine to bank, and how it also operated the elevator flaps on the tail plane for climbing and descending. Also, how to operate the rudder bar with our feet to make the aircraft turn. The use of the wing flaps on take-off and landing was also explained to us, as were the main instruments – the altimeter, the air speed indicator and the artificial horizon. We learnt how to start the engine and to taxi. Then came our first flight, with the instructor in charge, and the pupil having hands and feet lightly on the controls so as to appreciate the effects as they moved. The roles were then reversed, with the instructor correcting any errors. My first flight was on 23 January. That was after attending a funeral parade for two pupils who had collided a few days before our arrival. Another funeral parade was held a day or two later. Not an encouraging start, but it taught us that one had to be constantly alert and careful.

As it was January, the weather was not always right for flying light-weight Tiger Moths and we were told to expect an eight weeks stay, during which we would have to get in twelve hours flying before going solo. Weather permitting, we flew alternately in the mornings one day, and in the afternoon the next. At other times we attended courses on the same subjects as at ITW, with occasional sten-gun firing and bayonet practice. At night, there was a rota for guard patrols of four hours and twenty minutes around the perimeter of the airfield. We did this in pairs, carrying loaded sten-guns. A malevolent little flight lieutenant made a habit of cycling or walking round the airfield in the darkness to catch out any patrols who might be 'skiving' behind a hangar or sheltering from the cold winds. The first time I was on patrol, we saw him coming but we were correctly on patrol. We wished him goodnight and said we had nothing to report. By the time we were due for our second guard duty, we had learnt of his penchant and we decided to do something about it. We kept a careful watch, and round about 2 am we saw him on his bicycle some distance away. We hid behind a hut until he was close to us, and then jumped out with sten guns at his chest and shouts of 'Who Goes There?' We made him identify himself strictly according to the book and he failed to bother the patrols on the following nights!

On one wet Saturday afternoon when flying had been cancelled, I decided to go into Wolverhampton. As I approached the guard room to book myself out, I could see a WAAF standing outside. As I got nearer, I found it was Daphne. She had come to see me just for the afternoon, not even knowing if I was going to be free. It was one of those chance meetings which we had from time to time.

I enjoyed flying the Tiger Moth and it behaved so well for beginners. My instructor was a good one and that counted for a lot. He had one other pupil beside myself and after we had done roughly twelve hours flying he was ready to let us go solo. The procedure was for him to go with the pupil for a take-off, circuit and landing, and then to jump out and send the pupil up alone. He took my colleague up first and I was left waiting for their return. But before they got back, the Station Commander (who I had not met before) came over and said he would take me up.

I took off, with the CO sitting behind me, and began a circuit of the airfield at 1,000 feet. Suddenly, we ran into fog. I wasn't too worried, as I was turning on to my downwind leg and the fog seemed to be ahead on the course I was just leaving. The airfield was clearly visible. While still turning, another Tiger Moth appeared out of the fog a little way above me, also turning. It was probably my partner, returning. I began to dive and tightened my turn. There was a shout of 'I've got her!' in my headphones, and the CO wrenched the control column from my hands (there were dual controls) and with full opposite rudder we dived away in the opposite direction. It was there that the fog was thickest. We couldn't see a thing. The CO put the plane into a climb and we weaved about for several minutes with no visibility. He kept saying 'It should clear in a minute'. I suggested that if we had stayed on course, the landing ground would have remained visible and we could have got down, but the commander would have none of it. Before we took off he had told me he wanted to get some flying time in and I suspect it had always been his intention not to do just a single circuit with me. There were five tall industrial chimneys on the edge of the airfield so I was glad he had climbed. The chimneys have since been demolished (we didn't do it!) and we must have been well clear of them. The CO continued altering course in the hope of breaking out of the fog and at last we came out into beautiful sunshine at about 3,000 feet. Below us were lovely green fields. 'Do you know where we are?' he asked me. I told him I had never been this far from base. He decided to go lower and look for somewhere to land. There were sheep and horses in some fields, and others had been ploughed. At last, the CO spotted a field which seemed a possibility but I saw that although it appeared green and smooth, grass had grown over ploughed furrows. The CO went low and took a look. He said he thought he could land along the furrows. I was a bit apprehensive, but he did just that without us having a mishap. We came to a stop right at the end of the field, just before a collection of trees.

A farm worker from the next field had seen us and came running over with a pitchfork. We convinced him we were not Germans and asked him where we could telephone the flying school to let them know where we were. He directed us to a pub not far away and we left him with his pitchfork to guard the plane. I think he felt quite important.

At the pub, the landlord told us where we were and allowed the CO to use the phone. It was arranged that a van would be sent out to pick us up. The CO ordered a beer and some cigarettes and I had a ginger beer. He had no money on him, so I had to pay. It came to two shillings and eleven pence, and I had exactly three shillings in my flying suit.

While we were waiting in the pub, a police sergeant and a constable turned up, and treating it all very seriously, they took down full particulars. By then, it was about 1 pm and the landlord asked if we wanted lunch. The CO told him we had no more money, but in my inside pocket I always carried a ten shilling note for emergencies. This bought us a lunch of fish in parsley sauce, peas and potatoes, followed by prunes and custard. We were the only customers. I was thinking that my solo was becoming expensive but the CO promised to reimburse me when we got back. As no transport turned up, the CO phoned again and was told the fog had been too thick but one was now on the way. The CO bought more beer with the change from my ten shillings and with nobody else around I tinkered on the piano.

When the van finally arrived, the CO asked the driver about the fog, and was told that it had now completely cleared. Thereupon, he decided that he would fly back alone and I should go in the van. We went back to the field and with the help of the farm worker, who had had to go without his lunch, we turned the aircraft into the wind, and I swung the propeller and started the engine. The CO had to negotiate the ruts from a standing start but, with a good rev of the engine he began to move and with a number of hops was away.

On my return to the airfield, being now completely penniless, I went in search of the CO. He didn't seem to be about and at last I was told he had gone to hospital. I feared he had had an accident. 'Oh no! He's all right' I was told, 'but when you and he didn't come back, your own instructor took off to go and look for you. In the fog, he crashed into a house. He's in hospital with a broken leg and the CO has gone to see how he's getting on'.

I never saw my instructor again, and I had to wait several days before the CO sent for me to give me back my thirteen shillings. Meanwhile, I had been without funds. Perhaps the CO was also, and had to wait till he had claimed for his expenses!

I asked him about completing my solo, but he said he had passed me as qualified and I would be going to Canada to complete my training. I was given indefinite leave, during which I took Daphne to see Evelyn Laye in 'The Merry Widow' in London. Afterwards, we couldn't find anywhere to get a bite to eat and, in desperation, we went into the Charing Cross Station Hotel. We couldn't afford the price of their sandwiches, but the young waitress brought us some that a customer had not eaten. Air Force pay was such that we depended on charity.

CHAPTER NINE

Elizabeth Regina Molto Sic(k) Transit

My indefinite embarkation leave came to an end on 18 March, when I had to report to Heaton Park, Manchester. This was another 'holding' unit and I remained there for twenty-one days. As I could not travel from Reading on the 18th to be there at 8 am, I went up the day before and reported that afternoon. It was difficult to believe, but I was turned away! Apparently, I was not on the unit's strength until early the next morning, so the guard would not admit me! I had all my kit with me and they at least let me leave that there while I went back into Manchester to stay overnight at a hotel. In the evening, I treated myself to a trip to the theatre to hear Webster Booth and Anne Ziegler in 'The Vagabond King'.

The next day, I exchanged my comfortable hotel accommodation for a cold Nissen hut with a stone floor, beside a misty lake in Heaton Park. Being only a 'holding' unit, the usual RAF 'bull' existed, because nobody knew what to do with us. There were useless parades, cleaning and patrol duties and continual harassment. A 'Discipline Flight' was formed to which defaulters were transferred for extra drill and punishment chores. The fact that there were enough 'offenders' for the formation of a special flight was an indication of the way the unit operated. It was the easiest thing in the world to be put into the 'Discipline Flight' – buttons not shining, hair too long, marks on uniform, late for parade, and even looking too cheerful! How anyone could look anything like cheerful was hard to imagine. It was the old story of dim, regular NCOs persecuting the trainee aircrew and enjoying it.

Young lads of today would never stand for it, but it was very different in the 1940s. There was one barber on the camp, but he could not cope with the number of airmen who had been ordered to get haircuts, and we were unable to go off the site. Consequently further punishment was earned for defaulting an order to get one's hair cut!

We were being constantly chided for the white 'flashes' in our caps being dirty. It was impossible to get 'Blanco', and the water which came out of the taps, through rusty pipes was brownish. Perhaps it would have been better if we had washed them in the lake – but that was out of bounds. Possibly in case of suicide attempts!

Thankfully, on 8 April we were put on a train with all our kit, going we knew not where. There was a pay parade before we left, but my pay details had not come through. So I was off to Canada with only a bob or two in my pockets.

The train took us to the docks at Gourock, Glasgow, and we crossed the Atlantic in the *Queen Elizabeth*. No, not the luxury liner. She had been converted into a troop carrier. There were some rough seas, with waves which seemed to be about 100 feet high. Cadets were leaning over the side being sick and others crawling about looking green. Some of us had been given jobs to do and, being able to type, I was put in the Purser's office. It involved taking messages to different parts of the ship – out of bounds to other cadets – and it kept me busy so that I did not suffer with sea-sickness like many others.

The food on board was good, with real white bread instead of the dirty grey 'standard' loaf we had had in Britain for so long. Plus plenty of creamy milk and fresh fruit.

We set out at first with a convoy of smaller ships and some warships but after a day or so we left them behind, and saw only sea and sky. After eight days, the Statue of Liberty came into view and we docked in New York.

We were taken by train from there to Moncton in New Brunswick, Canada, via Boston.

CHAPTER TEN

A Land of Milk and ... Maple Syrup

At Moncton, a tremendous camp had been built with permanent two-storey wooden housing. The rooms were fitted with two-tiered bunks of a much superior type to those in Britain. Better still, we had soft mattresses instead of the hard, hair filled 'biscuits'. True, there were plain wooden floors which had to be scrubbed, but there were proper washrooms and showers WITHIN the buildings with plenty of hot water – a change from trotting out in the cold, half-naked, as we had done at Manchester and Ludlow.

The food was excellent, and on every table there were two large jugs, one full of ice-cold creamy milk, and the other with golden brown maple syrup.

We were allowed out without a pass until 12 midnight and until 2 am on Sunday mornings. But staying on the camp was no hardship as the site included its own cinema, theatre and church. Moncton itself was not very large, although classified as a city, with a cathedral. Apart from its tall tower, the cathedral was plain and uninteresting outside, but had a fine entrance hall, and the inside was most attractive. The streets had wooden sidewalks, and cars were plentiful, with no petrol shortage. Bicycles were scarce, possibly because they were taxed and carried number plates. Instead of Men's and Ladies' models, the bikes had a crossbar which dipped down near the saddle, thus being 'unisex'. Railway lines cut across roadways without any level-crossing gates, and the trains were pulled by steam engines equipped with cowcatchers, bells and sirens, which sounded like an air-raid warning starting up. A railway line ran right up to the border of the camp, and a tidal river, the Petitcodiac, flowed nearby. There were no pubs and although I was told there were liquor stores, I never saw one, and I cannot recall any drunkenness on the camp. There was no blackout, of course, and as darkness descended, one had to ignore the inclination to draw non-existent curtains!

After the shortages at home, it was like being in a new world to find shops full of oranges, lemons, apples, pears, milk, biscuits, razor blades, shampoos, cigarettes and cigarette lighters, ice cream and many rich foods. Chocolate was rarely available but no sweet coupons were needed. There were masses of magazines and fat newspapers – four pages only in Britain – but no bananas or silk stockings. Lisle stockings had become more usual. Woollen goods were expensive and we found that on items that RAF personnel wanted to send home, prices had been raised by the shopkeepers. We were able to send parcels back to the UK weighing 5lb to civilians, or 11lb to the Forces. I sent several of these to my parents and to Daphne so that they could enjoy things unobtainable at home – marmalade, chocolate, lard, peaches, banana flakes, raisins, Rinso and shampoo. My first 11lb parcel to Daphne went through all right, but the next one was returned with the explanation that the higher weight applied only to Canadian Forces overseas.

As I had not been paid before I left Manchester, I was short of cash at first, and we were given only four dollars on arrival. The cinema was free, so that was a help. Hand-drawn posters were put up outside to show what film was showing and one badly written poster went up with the last two letters of the final word transposed, and read – 'I MARRIED AN ANGLE'. A wit had added 'I hope she's ACUTE one'.

As this, again, was a 'holding' unit, we were mainly employed on odd jobs. I was on 'butchery', chopping and carrying sides of beef and delivering meat to the various Messes. My gory hands, boots and overalls were quite attractive – but only to the flies!

CHAPTER ELEVEN

Landing In Trouble

After just over three weeks at Moncton, a party of us was taken by train most of the way across Canada to a tiny spot called Bowden, about seventy miles north of Calgary, Alberta.

At Montreal, the train stopped and we were told there would be a two hour wait. I slipped out of the station and managed to fit in a visit to see my grandmother, two aunts, and two cousins who I had never met before.

From Montreal, the train wound its way past the northern edges of Lake Superior and then across the endless miles of flat prairie full of golden wheat. It was a wonderful sight, but it soon became monotonous as there was wheat and nothing else for as far as the eye could see. The train stopped again at Winnipeg, and we were given a welcome by a gathering of elderly and middle-aged ladies of evident Scottish origin. They had retained their Scottish accents and we laughed and talked while we tucked into delicious home-made cakes and scones which they had prepared.

We travelled in the train from the 9–17 May, and then caught a small train from Calgary to Bowden. Here, the station consisted of only a short, uncovered piece of raised concrete and nothing more. Nearby, were a few houses, not more than thirty, and some silos for storing the wheat.

A roadway ran north/south alongside the rail track, and on either side were fields and more fields. In one field there was a line of little trees and a wandering narrow stream. This was a useful landmark when flying as otherwise the fields were extensive with little to differentiate them.

Some service transport took us from the concrete platform to the airfield which was about a mile away. We began flying the next day. The aeroplane in use was the Fairchild Cornell, a single engine, low-wing monoplane which gave better flying visibility than the Tiger Moth biplane. It handled much the same, but faster.

We had long hours of duty. Reveille was at 5 am with flying starting an hour later, followed by breakfast from 8 to 8.30. Flying then continued until lunch at 1.00 pm. In the afternoon we did ground studies and instruction until 6 pm. On the following day, reveille was at 6 am with an early breakfast, after which there were ground studies until a 1 pm lunch, with flying from 2.00 to 9 pm. We were not flying all that time. Each instructor took groups of us up in turns, one by one during the flying period. We also did simulated flying in the Link Trainer on the ground. This thing was supposed to respond to the controls like a real aircraft, but it had a time lag which to my mind was not much help in learning to fly.

On 23 May, I received my first letter from home since leaving the UK on 5 April. Daphne was writing regularly and a whole batch arrived together a few days later. At the same time, my kitbag arrived. It had not been transferred from the luggage van at Calgary when we changed trains, and I had been without fresh clothing, study books and other requirements for two weeks.

By this time, my flying was going quite well except when landing on bright sunny days. In England we had used a grass airfield and all went well. But at Bowden, a brand new white concrete runway had been laid across a field. When landing, the glare from the white concrete caused me to be unable to judge my height correctly and often I had to make two or more attempts. Eventually, it was found that my eyes did not respond rapidly to changes of light and although dark goggles and green strips on the windshield were tried, it was decided that my eyesight would not allow me to finish the course.

It was the most miserable day of my life. I had set my heart on flying and I was devastated. I had realised quite early on that some days I was misjudging my height, and it began to dawn on me that this was only in bright sunshine. I had no idea that my eyes were to blame. I just thought that I was the cadet being sent up in an aircraft with a smaller undercarriage than the others – and with square wheels!

CHAPTER TWELVE

Short Cuts

Sadly, my piloting days had come to an end, and I remustered as a trainee navigator.

On 17 June, 1943. I left Bowden Flying School, and went to No. 3 MD (Manning Depot) at Edmonton, Alberta, where I joined a squad of British RAF cadets who, like myself, had failed their piloting course.

However, it was an RCAF (Royal Canadian Air Force) station and we were under RCAF jurisdiction. Our blue RAF uniforms were taken from us and we were issued with RCAF summer-khaki drill clothing. This was no bad thing, as the weather was extremely hot. However, we were persecuted by the NCOs. I had to have two haircuts in the same week. Fortunately, the camp barber charged only 25 cents, whereas it was 75 cents in the town.

For the first time since arriving in Canada, I was in a large city and, when not on special duties we were allowed to go into the centre. I took the opportunity to send more parcels home – tinned fruit to my parents, and Evan Williams shampoos and Tangee lipstick to Daphne. The shampoo and lipstick had become unobtainable in England, and I preferred Daphne to use Tangee because it did not come off. Thankfully. I had had a pay day before leaving Bowden.

My visits to the city gave me my first experience of mixing with Canadian civilians. I was struck by the jazzy ties and dazzling jackets worn by the men, and by the bright lipstick and red nails of the females. Gum chewing by both sexes was never ending.

Letters from Daphne were taking longer to reach me because of my move to Edmonton, and the censor usually opened them. On 29 June, I got one, uncensored, telling me of the deaths of Leslie Howard, the actor, and Leslie Heward, the conductor of the Halle Orchestra, for whom I had high regard. One of Daphne's letters was returned to her by the censor because she had asked me to send her some Goya Gardenia perfume. Apparently, such requests were not allowed – or perhaps the censor thought it was some sort of code!

Clothes could not be washed on the station. We suspected the NCOs had come to an arrangement with the Chinese running the laundries. Perhaps they also had something 'going'; with the camp barber!

On 3 July we were posted to our Navigation School in Edmonton, only to find that they were not ready for us. We were given seven days leave so usually I went swimming in the local baths, and had a midday snack of milk-shake, pumpkin pie and apple pie which seemed to be the staple fare on all the menus.

CHAPTER THIRTEEN

Beware of the Bull!

No. 2 AOS (Air Observers' School) was situated on the aerodrome on the outskirts of Edmonton, and we began our training there on 10 July. Twenty-five of us were RAF cadets, plus one Australian, and one New Zealander. We were joined by three RCAF cadets and we all became Course 80 N1.

We worked in pairs, sitting at school-type desks, doing all the usual flying subjects, with particular emphasis on navigation, maths, and meteorology. We did physical training outside every day and played basketball on a gravel court. I fell during one game and skidded along on my hands, tearing off skin and flesh. With my hand bandaged, my partner, Les Seaward, had to help me out with my navigation plotting for a while. He and I flew together as first and second navigator, alternately, with civilian pilots, in Avro Ansons.

We made our first flight on 19 July. It was a familiarization flight of 1 hour 40 minutes with each of us dong 50 minutes navigation, while the pilot showed us some of the wonderful surrounding scenery. We were only a little way from the eastern edge of the Rocky Mountains, and to the north, there were high craggy hills with dense, pine-clad down slopes and green valleys alongside the River Athabaska and The Lesser Slave Lake.

It was an almost unbelievable change from the area round Bowden where, for over 300 miles from Calgary to Edmonton, there was nothing but open, green flat country, with an occasional clump of trees, and one straight road running north/south beside the railway. Roughly, every thirty miles, there was a raised, uncovered concrete railway station platform, near wheat silos, a few houses, and some wooden barns.

As we were at an Observer School, we not only did navigation, but also air photography and reconnaissance. Many times we flew south, over this unremarkable terrain, instead of flying over the picturesque scenery to the north and west, presumably to test our navigation skills as all the fields looked alike, and there were no useful landmarks. When we flew at night, the lights at Jasper could be seen to the south-west, but otherwise there was darkness. We navigated largely with the help of radio beams picked up by the aircraft's DF (Direction Finding) loop aerial, and by taking frequent sextant shots of the moon, stars and planets. We had to ask the pilot to hold a steady course and altitude while taking these shots or an incorrect ground position would result. Radio beams coming from acute angles would also be liable to give a wrong position.

In addition to real air navigation, we did simulated navigation, in special classrooms fitted with moving plotting arms over a map, to indicate an aircraft's movement over the ground. The instructor could cause deviations of the arm, to introduce changes in wind speed or direction which the pupil had to recognize and make course alterations. If a pilot took evasive action from searchlights, fighters or ground defences, the navigator had to take this into account and not regard the deviation from track as being due to drift from a wind change.

Our course leader (Instructor) was a Flight Lieutenant Jones of the RCAF. He was an excellent instructor and we built up a good rapport with him. We were all willing and keen, and he admired our purposeful insistence for logical reasoning. We were learning from him, and he was learning from us.

The course lasted five months and in that time we did twenty daytime navigation flights and twelve at night. We rarely flew with the same civilian pilot, some of whom were surly or difficult to bond with. Some tended to be deliberately obstructive and caused navigational problems. However, quite early on I flew with one who chatted sociably before take-off, and who was interested in that I had come off a pilot's course. On the homeward leg of the flight, while my partner, Les Seaward, was doing the navigation, he called me up to the front and let me fly the Anson. It was a beautiful sunny morning, so, wisely, he didn't let me land it!

It was an extensive course and we had little time to ourselves. We were continually taking tests, and evenings were taken up fully with three hours homework or study, followed by some astro work with our sextants in the darkness. There was no cinema or theatre on the site and we could not leave the station. A rest room was available, where a voluntary organisation called The Knights of Columbus provided free stationery for letter writing. I wrote to Daphne every few days, and she usually managed to write even more frequently. We used air letter forms or airgraphs. The latter was photographed after posting, and delivered in reduced size (to save paper), so the writing had to be tiny enough to get all one wanted to say on the single sheet, yet large enough to be readable at the other end. Postage was ten cents from Canada, and six old pence from the UK. Those letters meant much to us while we were apart.

We were compatible in many ways and, often, when one of us did something, or thought of something, the other could match it. I broke my big toe playing football in Edmonton, and, at the same time, Daphne was in hospital having bones in her foot reset after the toe-arch had collapsed.

Shortly after this, we even managed to be put on a 'charge' at the same time. In Daphne's case she developed tonsillitis during a weekend visit home and had to be admitted to Station Sick Quarters at an Air Force unit in Reading. She was granted so many days sick leave, but when that had expired, she felt too weak to return to Gloucester and the MO at Reading gave her a certificate to take back with her the following day. But by that time, she had been reported absent and wheels had been set in motion to charge her. So despite having returned with her certificate she was marched into the presiding officer, under escort, and had to give an explanation. She was still feeling groggy and was quite upset about being disciplined unfairly. She was remanded until all enquiries could be made to ascertain the facts, when, of course, the charge was dismissed. Numerous people had been put to lots of trouble – all because everything had to be done by the book.

It was a case of 'BEWARE OF THE BULL!'

In my case, the instructor had sent Les Seaward and myself out to the aerodrome control tower to take sextant shots. A room at the top of the tower had observation windows in it, and we set to work. A door led out on to a flat roof with railings round it, and I suggested we went out there to avoid refraction from the window glass. In a matter of minutes the squadron leader (Admin) came bounding up the steps and out on to the roof, breathless and red in the face. He demanded our identity cards and told us we would be charged for being out of bounds. (Actually, having reached the top of the steps, he was the one out of 'bounds'!). I explained to him why we were there and since there was no notice about not going on to the roof, how were we to know. But this officious twerp would not be diverted from his determination to charge us. Not for him, the straightforward way of giving us a warning and a 'don't do it again'. We had to be put on a charge.

We reported back to our instructor and waited for a summons from the Station Warrant Officer – although, unaccountably the RCAF called him sergeant major. Our instructor had not heard about the observation roof being out of bounds, so that evening I went to the guard room and asked to see Station Standing Orders. I was not allowed to take them away so I spent a long session going through them meticulously. Naturally, the SP (Station Policeman) on duty wanted to know what I was searching for, and he told me that there was nothing in Orders about the flat roof. However, he knew that some airmen had been charged in the past – he believed because of a verbal ruling well before our time. In the morning, I reported this to our instructor and I think he must have had a word with the squadron leader concerned. Next day we were summoned to the guardroom where, instead of being charged, we were handed back our identity cards and no more was said.

I was one of the few who avoided disciplinary action although it was easy to find oneself in trouble innocently or accidentally. We were beset with petty rules and regulations so there was a constant fear that one might be infringing some unknown restriction.

It was a matter of 'BEWARE OF THE BULL!'

On a rare occasion, I got away from the camp to go to a cinema in the city. When I came outside, it was such a lovely night that instead of boarding the streetcar that was waiting, I decided to walk a few blocks. The 'tram' passed me but I caught up with it a little further on. It was lying on its side, battered, and leaning against another one with which it had collided. Already, crowds were round it and I couldn't see if anyone was hurt. My concern was to get back to the aerodrome before my pass expired. I hurried on and tried to hitch a lift from passing cars, all of which had to pass the camp because there was only the one straight road. Eventually one stopped, clearly guessing why I was running, and he got me back with minutes to spare. Otherwise, the fact that there had been an accident would not have been an acceptable excuse. Indeed the word 'excuse' did not exist as far as we were concerned. You were either back on time or you were late.

Chapter Fourteen

Bull and Beef

After several months of continual study, exams and night flying, and taking astroshots until 2 am the strain began to show. Tension and headaches were common. On top of all this, we were finding it difficult to cope with the niggling RCAF regulations. We recognized that a certain amount of 'discipline' was necessary, but it needed to be tempered with reasonable fairness, logical purpose, justice, and common sense. Here we were entering the fourth year of the war, and about to become active participants, yet the RCAF was excessively concerned with 'bull'.

One member of the squad called a meeting which we all attended and it was decided that without it becoming a mutiny, we would offer some resistance. It began with a bit of British sarcastic humour, and two or three of us combined to produce a humorous newspaper for the benefit of the other members of the course, poking fun where it was needed. We gave a copy to our instructor as he was quite aware of how we felt. It was likely he would circulate it.

Our living quarters were separated from the classroom and the airfield by a fairly wide, but, by British standards, not a very busy road. The Canadians called it a Highway. We were crossing it constantly, but never with any problems or danger. Suddenly, traffic lights were installed, controlled by one of the SPs in the guard room, and we were forbidden to cross until the 'CROSS NOW' sign was shown. We sometimes had to wait unnecessarily, and the lights were hardly needed. We could only assume that the squadron leader had been so anxious to dash across and put someone on a charge that he had nearly been knocked down.

A day or so after the lights had been installed our instructor in the classroom wanted the rather serious, oldest member of the course to go over to the living quarters to fetch something. He made his way to the door, paused, and with a straight face asked – 'Will you come with me, Sir, and hold my hand and see me across the road?' By this time our instructor had discovered that we were a bit different from the other pupils he had had, and he took it all in good part.

We had to go along with the order to cross with the aid of the traffic lights, but our instructor persuaded the CO to let us do certain things the RAF way, after that we stacked our bedding in the RAF fashion. The inspecting NCO then ripped it all down. We protested en masse and got permission to use the RAF style. Next, we refused to do RCAF drill movements, or to use the American terms for the parts of machine guns, and we stuck to the British phonetic alphabet when doing Morse or Aldiss lamp signalling and when using aircraft identification lettering.

It was only because of the irksome, illogical rules that we went to those lengths. Ridiculously, we were required to keep our text books and folders in our lockers in an order laid down in instructions, instead of in the order we needed to use them. That was soon changed.

When it came to night flying, the routes were being frequently changed after we had spent time on plotting our charts before take-off, and we were then expected to start all over again and still be ready to take off at the original time. That didn't last. We reworked our plans and went out to our aircraft when WE were ready. This annoyed the pilots who, being civilians, wanted to get back and go home without being delayed. In order to do this, some used to take short cuts so as to land at the time they had planned. It ruined our navigation, so we had that stopped.

The simulated flights which we did on the ground were done in windowless classrooms and, as most of these exercises were supposedly night flights we did not object to working in darkness with small, dim table lights – just as if we were doing the real thing. But if we were doing a daylight synthetic flight we objected to working in the dark. No one had objected before, but we insisted on having the classroom lights switched on. It was simply logical!

Only three members of the course failed to graduate and on 26 November 1943 we went on parade and were awarded our three stripes and our Observers' brevets. The latter was known as the Flying O – or the Flying . . . hole. There followed our Graduation Dinner, with good food and good speeches and our instructor announced that we had 'shaken him rigid' but he respected the reasoning behind all the 'upsets' we had caused.

We produced our final humorous newspaper for which I did a poem called 'Oh! Canada'. (see next chapter).

I came of age (twenty-one) just before the end of the course and some six weeks later I received a twenty-first birthday card from Daphne. I am sure my parents and my brother would also have sent cards but no others arrived.

I was awarded a Second Class Navigation Certificate, having qualified in nine subjects on ground work and six on night flying.

CHAPTER FIFTEEN

Per Ardua
Ad-Verse City

OH! CANADA!

After nearly a year, you'd no doubt like to hear
What I think of this land in the West.
So give me some time and I'll give you a rhyme
Pointing out all the things I hate best!

The rooms are so hot, you become a grease spot
While outside the temp'rature's low
And you'll soon catch a cold if you try to be bold
Going into the warmth from the snow.

A man is a 'guy', though I don't know quite why,
And something that's novel is 'cute',
While 'perty' means pretty – if out to be witty
'Period' is a good substitute.

And then it's a rule to call program(me) – 'skedule'
And to emphasis always say 'ever'.
If it seems awf'lly funny say 'dough' and not 'money'
Use slang if you want to be clever.

'Trams' are called 'streetcars', and 'restaurants', 'milk bars'
The High Street is called 'The Main Drag'
And 'sidewalk' means 'pavement', – (for us there's enslavement)
And a 'dame' that you hate's an 'old Bag'.

The chemist's the 'drug store', the pub is the 'jug store'
And mid-day is always called 'noon'
And 'auto' means car, and 'a walk' 'isn't far'
While a symphony's known as 'a toon'.

They think you are rum, if you're not chewing gum,
You're a most peculiar bloke
And if you drink beer, expect them to sneer,
For Canadians always drink 'coke'.

I'm calling sweets 'candy', and say 'fine and dandy'
I'm gradually learning the talk,
I now say 'tomayto' and French fried potato.
And eat all my food with a fork.

A smart chap's a 'dude', and to swear isn't rude
Your trousers are known as your 'pants'.
It can give you a fright when they say 'You're DAMN right'
And that word rarely gets a shocked glance.

So, as you can see, words meant nothing to me
When I first set my foot in this place,
But now I can swear without turning a hair
And still look you straight in the face!

CHAPTER SIXTEEN

Off Home and Off Balance

We left navigation school as sergeant observers on 28 November 1943, travelling by train from Edmonton, via Winnipeg, to Montreal, where the engine broke down. It would take two days to repair it, so we were given forty-eight hours freedom to do as we wished. I spent two glorious days with my aunts and three female cousins. My male cousin was in the Canadian Forces in the UK and, although I did not know it then, I was also going to see him quite soon.

With the engine repaired, we travelled on to Moncton, once again, but we stayed only one week. At 2 am on the morning of 14 December we began the journey back to Britain. The ground was covered in thick, crisp snow, and the temperature was well below zero. We marched down, with all our kit, to the railway line beside the border of the camp and waited in the bitter cold for our train. This took us to Halifax, where we waited once again on the exposed dockside before boarding a small ship which took us out to the liner on which we were going to cross the Atlantic. It was the *Mauretania* and our journey was not without incident.

By the time we had been taken aboard, both of my ears were frostbitten and swollen with blisters full of liquid. I found the ship's doctor and had to see him each day and have my ears painted with some white powdery liquid which was probably some form of boracic liniment. The sick bay, the toilets and the mess room were the only parts of the ship I saw. The ship was overloaded, and we were unable to move from the deck assigned to us. I was on one of the lower decks which was stripped bare of everything from one side to the other. Portholes were blacked out and kept closed. Some electric light bulbs hung on cables from the ceiling and swung about as the ship moved. Some lads were in hammocks, slung between posts, but most of us lay side by side on the wooden floor, fully dressed for the whole trip, with our kitbags and packs as our pillows. There were no blankets, but it was hot down there, and we lay so close together that it was almost impossible to get to one's feet. Not that we had anywhere to go; except for essential jaunts we stayed put all day and all night.

Just before reaching Liverpool – although down below, we had no idea where we were – the lights suddenly went out, and the ship shuddered, and keeled over at a sharp angle. People in hammocks fell out and crashed down onto those lying below. We could feel the ship twisting and turning and we learnt later that she was taking evasive action from a submarine attack. Happily, we continued safely.

On disembarking at Liverpool docks, I discovered that I had lost my balance. Whether this was due to the frostbitten ears or to the movement of the ship while lying prone for days on end, I was never sure. I had difficulty in walking in a straight line, or when turning my head. While waiting for our train, I had to ensure that I was not too near the edge of the platform. We went by train to Harrogate, and then by lorry to Ashville College at Pannal Ash, a few miles out of town.

It was 22 December, and as this was only a holding unit, we expected to be allowed home for Christmas. But the RAF doesn't work like that. We just hung about with absolutely nothing to do. There were no guard duties, or disciplinary restrictions apart from staying put. There was just a morning and evening parade to make sure we were all there. This was probably a good thing from my point of view, as I was still off balance. The drawback was that there was no sick parade and no treatment for my ears. After a whole week of doing nothing, we were suddenly sent on leave on 29 December. This release was without any warning, but the shock was even greater when we were told we did not have to return until 26 January!

On arriving home. I found my Canadian cousin was on leave and was staying with my parents for the next nine days. Daphne also got leave for the weekend 1–2 January. My parents did not know I was coming, and I am not sure how they managed with the food rationing.

My giddiness was still a problem and the fact that I was so unusually withdrawn caused Daphne to wonder whether after being apart for over nine months, things might have cooled between us. Plus, of course, I had to share my time not only with her but also with my parents and my cousin. However, after my cousin had returned to his unit, she managed to get fourteen days leave to be with me and things were back to normal. I took her to London to see Ivor Novello's 'Arc de Triomphe' and an enjoyable 'Cinderella' pantomime, followed by an introduction, for her, to opera on three successive nights when we saw 'Madam Butterfly', 'La Boheme' and 'Rigoletto'.

The Air Force still had no plans for me and I got a telegram extending my leave until 9 February. This was just as well, because I would not really have been fit enough to fly. Daphne got another weekend pass for 5 and 6 February, and by this time my blisters had healed and my balance was much improved.

On my return to Harrogate, our party was moved to the requisitioned Grand Hotel overlooking the Valley Gardens which were full of newly blooming daffodils, tulips and polyanthus. A stupendous, uplifting sight.

However, it was bitterly cold and I was put into an unheated room on the fifth floor. The hotel stood on a hill in an exposed position, and the cold winds made my room seem like an ice-box. A hit song by Vera Lynn was called 'Room 504' and this was the number of my room. I had not forgiven her for preventing me from going on leave at the end of my first week in the Air Force by wanting an audience of airmen in her film 'We'll Meet Again'. The room number brought it all back to me. However, it was unfair of me to link her with the coldness I had to suffer.

By a stroke of good fortune, I found a Forces Club Canteen which had a fire burning, and so that was where I spent many of my off duty evenings. When we complained about the cold, we were sent on long marches and given drilling, and in case we ever came down in the sea, we went a couple of times to a cold water swimming bath to do dinghy drill.

Nobody seemed to know why we were at Harrogate, or what to do with us. After a time, we were sent to a Naval College to study ship recognition – Allied ships and German ships – and to learn about the different compartments of torpedoes. We supposed we were being prepared to go to Coastal Command. But this training ceased and we went on a physical training course, where most of us were marked only 'fair'. It seemed they were looking for circus acrobats rather than navigators.

CHAPTER SEVENTEEN

Unwanted and Unpaid

On the 22 February, 1944 we were all sent to No. 22 Aircrew Holding Unit at Kirkham, situated between Blackpool and Preston. It was an extremely large and open camp, with strict security guards to prevent airmen slipping out without passes. It was also a long way outside the town where there were two cinemas, but there was a very big cinema on the site. We were housed in brick huts, each with a stove in the centre, but fuel was short, so the huts were rarely warm enough to linger in. My hut was about a mile from the main part of the camp, near to a high hedge which formed the furthermost border from the guarded main entrance. On a reconnaissance I discovered a hole which I used many times to get to a Post Office at Freckleton to mail letters and to withdraw money from my Post Office Savings account.

We had a few classes on Morse code, aircraft recognition, gunnery, anti-gas measures and talks on hygiene, but mostly we were given jobs on camp construction and defence (guard patrols). We were virtually just passing the time away once again. Not knowing what to do with us, we were immediately given a thirty-six hour pass on our second day! I managed to let Daphne know, and despite having only a few hours, we both went to our respective homes in Reading.

On 4 March Daphne was visiting a former friend from the Ministry of Health office in Reading but who was now in the Birmingham office. I slipped away through my hole in the hedge and caught a train to Birmingham. As I made my way out of the station I saw an SP coming towards me. Having no pass, I had to think quickly, and I boldly went up to him and asked him if he could tell me which platform for the Preston train. It worked, and I was not asked for my pass. On my return journey the next day, I waited at the station until the SP was distracted and successfully returned to camp via my hole.

As we were not really needed on the camp, I was able to get an official pass for the weekend 11/12 March when Daphne was going to stay at the home of a WAAF friend in Nottingham. I had not received any pay since my arrival and did not have the money for the fare. Thankfully the hole in the hedge allowed me to slip out to the Freckleton Post Office and withdraw some. On my return journey, I had a long wait at Manchester so I wandered around and found a simply marvellous YMCA with a downstairs restaurant staffed by about forty cheerful young girls as volunteer waitresses.

Being so numerous, they had time to stop and chat (the main reason for them being there!) and it certainly brightened up my wait. In view of my cash shortage, I was astounded and delighted when they told me my meal would only cost a shilling. My train was late coming in to Manchester and I did not get back to camp till after midnight. I was too tired to walk several miles to the Freckleton side of the camp and use my hole, so I reconnoitred the guard room from a distance and, as it was an aircrew sergeant on duty and not one of the SPs, I was able to slip in without being charged for my late return.

A few days later, I met up with Freddy Fish who had been on my navigation course in Canada. With our different postings, I had become separated from most of my earlier companions and I knew very few on the Kirkham camp. I had worked with Freddy on the humorous newspapers we had produced at Edmonton, and it was Freddy who had drawn the cover picture for the menu brochure for our Graduation Dinner. Freddy had been given six days CB (confined to barracks) for some misdemeanour, so I stayed in with him and played billiards every evening except one, when I made use of my hole and nipped in to Blackpool to see Bruce Trent in 'The Student Prince', at the New Opera House. CB, incidentally, was a misnomer for we were all confined to the camp unless given a pass; the punishment really meant continually reporting to the guard room.

During my trip into Blackpool, I tried to buy a razor as mine had been stolen, and I was using one I had borrowed from our friend in Birmingham. No razors were available, so I wrote to Gillette who replied that none were being made during wartime as they were making things of greater National importance. Unfortunately, the Air Force had not been told, and expected us to be clean shaven.

Through Daphne being in the RAF Record Office at Gloucester, she found that I was 'on loan' to Kirkham and my parent station was still Harrogate. My pay was being sent there and not forwarded. A visit to the Kirkham Admin Office put that right, but who knows how long that would have gone on if it were not for Daphne.

As it happened, we were about to be posted, although there was one last job assigned to Freddy and me. We were detailed to clear a vile, stagnant ditch and drain it to a nearby stagnant pond, and then to a lower pool below the camp. The stench was awful, and our feet were covered with thick black gunge. We sank into it, and the sucking, stinking, gurgling morass was reluctant to allow us to move. Poor Freddy lost his balance and fell back, right into it!

We never finished the job, for two days later, we moved to our new station. At last, we were going to our Advanced Flying unit to do what we had joined up to do. Since qualifying as navigators, December had been taken up by travelling back to Britain and January, February and March had been completely wasted. But not wasted so far as Daphne and I were concerned.

CHAPTER EIGHTEEN

All Fouled Up

On 29 March 1944 we were posted to No. 9 AFU at Llandwrog, an airfield on a sandy promontory in North Wales. The letters 'AFU' stood for Advanced Flying Unit, although a more usual translation was 'All Fouled Up', or with a substituted 'F' word.

On arrival, we were informed that it was a twenty-four hour working day, and certainly we got little sleep. It was pretty primitive and miles from habitation. We lived in unheated huts within fifty yards of the sea, and separated from it only by sand dunes and a minefield. There was no water on the site and the lavatories consisted of two buckets.

We were awakened by the Tannoy loudspeaker in the hut at 6.30 am. With nowhere to wash or shave, we simply dressed and made our way to a roadway where 'Liberty Buses' ran at 6.45, 7.00 and 7.15 am to the main camp. This was three miles away – a 10 minute journey. Unwashed, we ate breakfast in the Mess and then crossed the road to an ablution hut which was used by all personnel from AC2 upwards. There were eighteen tin bowls and seven mirrors and shaving had to be a quick process to make way for others. Next door was a proper toilet block.

By 8.00 am we were expected to be on the roadside to catch the buses to our classrooms, classes being from 8.15 to 12.15 pm. We returned by bus for dinner at 1.00 pm, and caught buses back to the classroom at 1.40 for classes at 2.00 pm. Food was sparse and not very satisfying, so dinner was soon eaten and, with luck, one could have a wash, and collect and mail post before catching the bus. We worked from 2.00 until 6.00 pm and caught the 6.15 bus back to the Mess. I found I could fit in a shave after tea instead of having to contest for a bowl or mirror in the morning, as long as I hurried, as the bus left again at 7.15 pm for more classes at 7.30. We usually got back to our cold hut by the sea by 9.30 pm.

We were allowed one day off a week, but the last bus back from Caernarfon left at 9.00 pm, so a cinema or evening entertainment was not possible. I went into Caernarfon only once. I had no desire to go again. The natives were downright unfriendly – ignoring the airmen when they went into shops, and pointedly speaking only in Welsh. There was no point in going again. (Racial discrimination is not a new disease).

It was nearly four months since I had last flown, and in all that time our stripes and brevets seemed to have qualified us only for menial general duties and hanging about. At last, it appeared that despite the spartan conditions, our long days in the classrooms were preparing us for proper service to the war effort, as navigators. On 31 March, it was announced on the radio that the RAF had lost ninety-six bombers (about six hundred lives) the previous night, and perhaps that was why we were at last going to be needed. The target had been Nuremberg and it was the biggest Bomber Command loss on a single raid in the war.

We began flying on 6 April and we were warned of the proximity of Snowdon with a height of 3,560 feet and frequently covered by mist. To put our minds at ease, we were told that there was a mountain rescue team based at the main camp, and they had never yet failed to locate missing bodies!

The weather was atrocious all the time we were there and although we flew over the Isle of Man a number of times, the cloud was so dense, I never saw it once.

We flew in Avro Ansons piloted by civilian pilots, with two trainee navigators to a plane. My first flight on 6 April (Maundy Thursday) was on a route via Worcester, Leominster and Crewe. On the way, my second navigator was airsick and brought up his dinner all over my charts. We flew over Northern Ireland on Easter Sunday when the weather was clearer and it was interesting to see the Irish scenery for the first time.

We navigated largely with the aid of the DF (direction finding) loop bearings from radio stations, and by picking up pulses on a radar screen on the navigator's table. This was known as 'Gee', and it became our key navigation aid when on operations, backed up by another radar system called 'H2S'.

As a result of our living conditions, most of us were suffering from bad colds and using up handkerchiefs by the dozen. Paper tissues were not in existence in those days.

On Easter Monday we took off early on a route via Chester, Derby, Shrewsbury, Wellington, Crewe and Anglesey. Visibility was nil and the radio was not working. We navigated using information on winds supplied at the Meteorological briefing. As we came out of cloud, I recognized that we were right over Wolverhampton aerodrome where I had done my Tiger Moth training. Someone must have moved it for it was fifteen miles off our proper track!

When on early morning flying, we used to leave a note in the guard-room the night before, describing which hut we slept in, and the position of our bed so that the SP on duty could come round and wake us without disturbing the other occupants. The SP always came in through the front door, and left through the back. My note read – 'Nearest bed to rear door, on left going out'. One morning the SP came in by the rear door and began waking the wrong people. I awoke and called out 'Not that one – I'm the one on the left'. The SP looked at his piece of paper and said 'You're wrong, Sarge – it says here – "on the left", but your bed's on the right'. I replied 'It says on the left GOING OUT'. The SP looked at his paper once again and looked a bit puzzled. Then, to satisfy himself that he hadn't made a mistake, he told me 'Ah! Well – I'm coming in you see!'

Thereafter, I had to stipulate which door determined the bed.

Sleep was important. On one night, I took off at 8 pm and returned at 11.00, taking off again at 3.30 am for another three hours, although we had to return after half an hour as the aircraft IFF (Identification Friend or Foe) was not transmitting. This was a signal being constantly transmitted to ground stations to ensure that we would not be treated as an intruder.

On 14 April, I received an air letter which Daphne had posted to me whilst I was in Canada on 7 November, and several more written in November and December followed until mid-May.

With the constant study, flying and travelling everywhere by buses, I was not getting much exercise so, on our day off I decided to go for a run on the sands. On climbing up the sand dunes I found the tide was right in, so the run was off. On the way back, I came across some Aussies playing rugby, so I asked if I could join in. They agreed and told me it was Australian Rules. I guessed I would soon pick it up. But I found that it meant "anything goes'. I came away, bruised, battered and with a bleeding nose. With no water on the site, I had to stay dirty and blooded till the next morning. It was a case of 'playing' through the nose!

On our next night flight, we were briefed to fly at 4,000 feet and we decided that we would be warm enough without our padded flying kit. But after take-off, we ran into thick, bumpy cumulonimbus cloud and the pilot climbed to 11,000 feet to try to clear the towering tops. Without oxygen, we couldn't go higher. Lightning was flashing around us and rain was coming in through poor sealing round the windows. We were absolutely frozen. In view of his twisting and turning the pilot abandoned the navigation exercise and we had to be guided back by radio and by a searchlight put up at the airfield. It was still raining and by the time we got back to our hut we were frozen and drenched.

On another occasion, we were to do practice bombing beside the River Severn near Gloucester. We passed over an aerodrome close to the RAF Record Office where Daphne worked, and I hoped the weather would be too bad to proceed so that we would have to land. But the weather was not co-operating! She wrote to me and reported that she had seen an aircraft flying by at about the time we were there and wondered whether I was up there. It was nearly another of those unplanned meetings.

For my last flight at Llandwrog I was made the Pathfinder, and my assistant navigator was a Peter Bloomfield. I knew that that was the name of the son of a couple who were friends of Daphne's parents who I had met once or twice, but I had never met their son. Now I was meeting him quite unexpectedly. We got on well, and the flight was a success. On landing, I suggested that we were bound to meet up again when the war was over. But it was not to be. Peter was shot down over Germany on an operational flight and although he was reported to have survived, we were told much later that German soldiers had taken him to a wood, ordered him to walk into it, and then shot him in the back.

Eight of us were the first to qualify on the navigation course and I was delighted when Freddy Fish and I were selected for posting to an aerodrome near Gloucester. We were the only southerners on the course so it was ideal. Right at the last minute, we were made to swap with a Yorkshireman and a Scot who had been allocated to Hixon in Staffordshire. Neither of them had any wish to go to Gloucester and we had no wish to go to Hixon, but the Air Force seemed reluctant to allow postings to home areas.

On my last day at Llandwrog, I received the Christmas card Daphne had sent to me in Canada. It was 24 April so this took only four months to find me. Things were improving.

As it was our last night on the camp, Freddy and I took ourselves off to the cinema for the only time since our arrival. There had been no opportunity before. Next morning, we were off to our new unit at Hixon.

CHAPTER NINETEEN

Daphne

Daphne had written to me nearly every day since my return to England. Occasionally she wrote of being fed up with the petty rules and regulations of the Air Force, but on the whole things were not too bad. She had been given permission to live off the camp in a private billet where she had more freedom and less interference. Her evenings and weekends were usually unrestricted. But even when she was living on the camp, there was a cinema on site and apart from one 'domestic' night she was free to go into Gloucester or Cheltenham to cinemas, dances, Forces Clubs, concerts or pubs. All in all, it was luxury compared to how aircrew were treated.

She was able to obtain thirty-six hour passes often at weekends, or forty-eight hours if I was going home too. On one occasion, she went to stay for the weekend with a friend at Blackpool. On the train, she changed out of uniform into civilian clothes, which was not allowed. On the return journey, she went to the toilet to change back again and found she had left her black tie behind. That meant trouble. When she got back to her compartment she noticed that the man opposite was wearing a black tie. She explained her predicament and he told her he had been to a funeral and he had another tie with him. She borrowed the black one and thus luckily avoided trouble on arrival at camp.

When the WAAF officer realised that several of the girls were disobeying the 'no civvies' regulation, she instituted a spot inspection. Hastily, the girls leant out of their hut windows and called out to the airmen in a hut opposite, who came over and picked up the civilian clothing as the girls tossed it out. The boys probably enjoyed the incident, as they did on another occasion when Daphne was cleaning the hut windows. She climbed out to sit on the sill to do the outsides, but she slipped off. Her skirt caught on the stud of the latch and she was left dangling with her skirt up to her waist and the boys opposite getting a surprise leg and bloomers show!

In October 1942, she took her Trade Test as Clerk GD (General Duties) and became a Leading Aircraftwoman (LACW) and was able to put up her 'props' (propeller badge). Shortly afterwards she was sewing a red chevron on one sleeve to denote War Service. It was never clear why this was necessary. We were all doing war service, and I don't recall seeing airmen or airwomen wearing such insignia. Perhaps at Gloucester the WAAFs wanted to brighten up their appearance for their hats were ghastly things. In later years they were allowed to wear berets or forage caps which gave them a much more cheeky look.

In earlier chapters I have made only passing mention of Daphne, but our lives were so much entwined that more needs saying about her and her background. Hence this chapter.

Once upon a time, there was this young girl who lived in Reading. She was not breathtakingly beautiful like heroines in novels or 'bodice-rippers'. But this is a true story.

On leaving school, she entered the Civil Service and had to travel by train to London where she worked in a big office. She had little chance of a social life after travelling home at the end of each day and she had no real boyfriends. But she enjoyed dancing on Saturday evenings.

Then came the war. The quiet pattern of her home life was cut short and she was whisked off compulsorily by her employer to a strange town many miles to the north. This was Blackpool. Away from parental control, she grew up rapidly and became independent. She discovered excitement with a capital 'E'.

She also discovered BOYS. She was able to indulge her delight in dancing by going nightly to either the Tower Ballroom or the Winter Gardens. There, she got to flirt with three young servicemen – Blackpool was filled by the Forces – and she managed to rotate meetings with each without the other knowing. The girls knew this as 'Playing the Field'. She was grief-stricken when all three were suddenly moved away, but before she could ensnare replacements she was herself transferred to a newly opened Regional Office of her Department in her home town of Reading.

She was, at first, unhappy at leaving behind her office friends, and the happy life she had enjoyed in Blackpool, and, at the earliest opportunity she took a holiday and went back there. She met a Polish airman who greatly impressed her by clicking his heels and bowing when he asked her to dance. But as before, she was not content with just one boy in tow. She secured the attention of a tall, fair-haired English airman, and lost her heart to him. They kept in touch after her holiday was over and met a few times, but it was wartime and one day his aeroplane did not come back.

Once more, life in Reading assumed the dreariness she had experienced before. That is, until the day she was asked to take part in a concert party rehearsal where she met a young lad from her own office who lived near her and who walked her home.

As this girl loved to dance, she persuaded this lad to take her to the local dance hall and tried to teach him to dance. He was pretty inept, but this meant the lessons had to go on for quite a long time! They became very fond of one another and when a vacancy arose in the girl's fire-watching squad, he volunteered to fill the gap. They used to sit up to the early hours listening to records and enjoying each other's company.

She found it tedious when he took her to hear Bach's Mass in B Minor, but she did not let this interfere with their meetings, and she was much happier when he took her to see the film 'Bitter Sweet'. As this lad, whose name was Don, was about to join the RAF, the song from the film 'I'll See You Again' – became 'their song'.

The girl joined the WAAF soon afterwards and they used to write to each other nearly every day. They were deeply in love. Don was sent overseas for his flying training for ten months and letters criss-crossed over the Atlantic day after day.

But while Don was being kept busy and his mind occupied with studying and exams, Satan was finding work for the girl's attention and she met another fellow with whom she went to dances regularly. She came to like him a lot, and it was a difficult time for her. Deep in her heart she knew that she loved Don, and it was as well that he returned when he did.

In the next four months, to April 1944, they saw a great deal of one another and grew even closer. Marriage was what they both wanted, but these were difficult times, and it seemed prudent to wait until the war was over. Being on only service pay Don had no savings towards the cost of a home and there was always the possibility that he would not survive to the end of the war. The girl found this unsettling and began to wonder whether Don really loved her. But there were many others in a similar situation. These young people were under a tremendous emotional strain, not helped by being apart and having vital responsibilities affecting the life or death of their colleagues. On an operational squadron it was noticeable how the performance of those with problems of the heart fell below their normal standards.

CHAPTER TWENTY

Crews: Cruise: Cruse

T hese words all sound the same, and although they seem to have nothing in common, there is a tenuous connection.

CREWS: Once the trainee aircrews had completed their basic training, they were posted to an Operational Training Unit (OTU) to be formed into their crews for their operational flying. I was posted to No. 30 OTU at Hixon, near Stafford on 30 April, 1944. There was no compulsion about who we crewed with. We were given time to get to know one another and to choose who we thought we would get along with. It was important that crew members were compatible and that they selected colleagues who gave the impression that they would be capable and stable.

I noticed that most of the fellows were young, and some of the pilots made me think that they might be 'show-offs' and take risks to satisfy their egos. Our future lives were going to be largely in their hands, so I was searching for someone who looked mature, solid and reliable. It wasn't easy to find anyone to fit the bill and most chaps had dashed round quickly and had formed their crews while I was still looking.

Eventually, I was approached by an air gunner who was looking for a navigator to complete the crew he had joined. His name was Ron Hales and I liked the look of him. He introduced me to the rest of his crew and the pilot, George Lee; he was about ten years older than the rest of us and married. This was what I was seeking and I joined their crew.

Our crew consisted of: George Lee, pilot; Don Feesey, navigator; Ray Forbes, bomb aimer; Max Leversha, wireless operator; Ron Hales, mid-upper gunner; and Peter Turley, rear gunner.

Two of the crew were Australians – Ray Forbes, the bomb aimer, who had done a navigation course, which I reckoned to be an advantage, and Max Leversha. They were flight sergeants; the rest of us were sergeants. Later, when we graduated on to four-engined aircraft we were joined by Ray Clarke ('Nobby') as our flight engineer. He was also a sergeant, and was always known as 'Nobby', and I was always known as 'Fizz'.

We all got along well and blended into a competent and reliable team. That was not always the case with some crews.

CRUISE. At Hixon, we flew in Wellingtons – the twin engined aeroplane, not the boots! As part of our operational training we did 'circuits and bumps' (take-offs and landings), navigation exercises and gunnery and bombing practice.

There was training on the ground as well and as, at times, some members of the crew were not available for flying duty, pilots were allowed to go up with a part crew, as long as they always had a navigator and a gunner. On one occasion, we were due to go on a practice bombing run, and both our gunners were engaged on gunnery duties in the armoury. So that we could get on, I volunteered to fly in the rear turret and do the navigation from there. We were only going a few miles to a bombing range on Cannock Chase and, having been there earlier, I knew I could find the way there and back, without trouble. So we took off, with a crew of pilot, navigator cum rear gunner, and the bomb aimer.

All went well at first, but as we did a subsequent bombing run from the north, my intercom failed. The pilot could not hear me and I could hear only fragments of his words. We did the bombing run and instead of turning for a repeat attack, the pilot continued to fly southwards. He had every confidence in my navigation and was evidently waiting for his next instructions.

Finding that the intercom was not working, I decided to open the sliding doors of the turret and climb back into the fuselage. The doors refused to move. I tried repeatedly and kept working on my microphone. No joy with either. I watched the ground passing away below as we continued to fly south. 'Surely' I thought, 'George will realize that something is wrong and turn, or send Ray Forbes back to see what is wrong'. But we flew on. I saw Bournemouth appear behind us, and then the Isle of Wight. I kept looking round, expecting to see a fighter plane checking up on us, but we were completely alone in the sky. We flew on towards France. It was a beautiful day. The sun shone down from a clear blue sky on to the calm, shimmering water. Everything was peaceful and it was hard to believe that we were at war. It was a gorgeous afternoon at the end of May and apart from my anxiety as to where we were going to finish up, I was quite enjoying our seaside excursion.

At last, the plane began to turn. I imagine the pilot had discussed the situation with the bomb aimer and decided that a day trip to France might not be wise. He sent Ray back to my turret. Ray peered through the glass panel in the doors, and I demonstrated how they would not open. He was speaking to me through his intercom but I could hear nothing. He tried to open the doors from his side, but they would not budge. We looked at each other helplessly.

Suddenly my intercom crackled into life and I heard George asking Ray if he could tell him the course to get back to base. I called out that my intercom was now working but I was still unable to get out of the turret. Fortunately, with a good idea of the English countryside, I was able to direct George directly back to Hixon without any maps.

It was probably ice in the intercom system which had caused the communication problem, but it hardly seemed possible that ice would have jammed the doors. On landing, Ray came back and tried to let me out but the doors still failed to open. I was left sitting there until they found an armourer. He climbed aboard, applied his magic touch, and I was free. He had no idea why the doors had stuck. I was just thankful that nothing unpleasant had happened while we were in the air. If the plane had gone down, I would have gone with it. But it was a super cruise!

CRUSE. It was not unknown for aircrews on operations to have a sudden, uncontrollable need to relieve themselves. An Elsan toilet was fitted for such purposes, but it was not possible for the pilot to leave the controls and use it. We discovered that George had fitted a tin beneath his seat, with a funnel and tube leading into it. One night, Ray Forbes disconnected the tube and inserted a cork. The Bible, (First Book of Kings), tells of the 'widow's cruse' – an endless supply that never fails. And so it was for George! He had become somewhat overbearing and officious on getting a commission, and Ray had decided to do something about it.

CHAPTER TWENTY-ONE

Ditching and Getting Ratty

After the Spartan conditions we had experienced at most other RAF units, Hixon was something out of this world. It had a dining hall with flowers on the tables, and the food was excellent and plentiful. There was a separate Mess building with a bar, a games room with table tennis and billiards facilities, a writing room with several tables and chairs and two ante-rooms, one with a radio and one with a piano. It led us to believe that, as aircrew, we would have something like it at all future stations. In fact, we never saw anything like it again.

We were surprised at first to find how little the games room was being used, until we found that time for relaxation was rare. For the first two weeks we attended lectures and studied our respective subjects, the navigators being especially busy. We worked from 8 am until 6 pm, Sundays included, with no day off. Flying came later.

We did First Aid, and we went into a decompression chamber to appreciate how lack of oxygen affected one's behaviour. Here, we were given simple arithmetic tests to be done without oxygen and, although the answers we came up with were absolutely absurd, we insisted that they were right. We played a card game with one crew member having no oxygen, and he was sure he was playing the Queen of Hearts when it was really the nine of Clubs. (Even without oxygen starvation, some Bridge players have been known to do the same thing!). It made us realise how the safety of the whole crew could be threatened if just one of us should ever be affected with an oxygen supply failure.

George Lee, our pilot, went solo in the Wellington on 15 May. Poor Freddy's pilot was taken off training, having failed to make satisfactory landings but Freddy was lucky to be able to join another crew almost immediately. Happily, all the members of that crew successfully came through a full operational tour of duty, and survived the war.

Once the pilot had 'soloed', we rose at 6.30 am, breakfasted at 7.15 and reported to the Flight Office at 7.40. We drew our flying kit, changed into it, and were taken by buses to the aerodrome, where the navigators received their briefing and meteorological details, and drew up their route charts ready for take-off at 10 am. When airborne, the navigator was kept busy checking the aircraft's position every few minutes with loop bearings from radio stations, taking and plotting sextant readings, obtaining the 'Gee' radar pulses on his monitor screen and converting these to give 'fixes' on his chart. From these, he could measure the difference between the compass course and the track taken over the ground (the drift due to a wind change) and calculate new wind speeds and direction and a new course for the pilot to fly to return to the official track.

The navigator worked in a little cubby-hole with a dim table light, and he had to avoid being distracted by the crackling in his headphones, the conversations between other crew members, and the freezing coldness. Trivial conversations in the air were banned, but the pilot would call up each member in turn to check that he was all right and not suffering from oxygen or intercom failure.

On landing, the buses took crews back to the Flight Office where they were questioned about the flight (debriefing) and the behaviour of the aircraft and the various instruments.

Sometimes we did cross-country navigation exercises, practised high level bombing, or did fighter affiliation, when we would undergo a mock attack by a Hurricane (actually an adapted Defiant) and the pilot would have to dive and twist (corkscrew), causing more problems for the navigator. At other times, the gunners would get firing practice at a drogue being towed by another aircraft – possibly a Hurricane or a Lysander – and we all had constant aircraft identification sessions.

We also had to practise 'ditching' procedures – 'ditching' meaning to come down in the sea ('the drink'). We practised in a large pool on the base, where we used an aircraft fuselage and wings moored to a jetty. In a nearby wooden shack, we stripped and put on PT shorts and plimsolls. We then put on wet canvas flying suits which had been used by a previous team, and 'Mae West' lifejackets.

We took up our normal positions in the fuselage, and when the pilot shouted 'Prepare for ditching' we moved to our ditching positions to brace ourselves against the imagined impact of hitting the water. On the shout of 'Abandon aircraft!' we inflated our Mae Wests and exited at the various points allocated to each member of the crew. The rubber dinghy had to be extracted from its storage position in the wing, inflated and floated. At first we got into it directly from the wing, but after that we had to jump into the water with the dinghy upside down and learn how to right it and clamber in from the water. This was not easy. Once aboard, the wireless operator had to get out the emergency radio and crank the handle to send out a distress signal.

You may think we had a lovely time splashing about, but the fun soon wore off. The Mae Wests had blocks of green dye in them so that the ditched airmen could be spotted by the air-sea rescue people. Thus, the pool was covered in the dye from repeated practices and the water was pretty stagnant and filled with weeds. Yet we were not alone in the smelly pool. As we were trying to clamber into the dinghy, a couple of dead rats floated by! A guaranteed way of providing the incentive to get aboard the dinghy as quickly as possible.

After we had practised ditching several times, we were allowed to go back into the changing hut and discard our wet flying suits and dry ourselves. Our bodies smelled pretty awful, but there was nothing we could do about that. We dressed and walked back to the ablutions block where we could shower.

The following day, we were given seven days' leave. (I didn't realize we smelled that bad!) However, we were unable to get away on time as we could not get our passes signed until late in the afternoon. I travelled to Kings Cross with Ron and Peter, who were both taken ill on the train with diarrhoea. We had had liver for dinner and we thought perhaps it was 'off'. We arrived in London at midnight and found all the tube trains and bus services had stopped. Ron and Peter found a taxi to take them to Charing Cross and I got one to Paddington as the RTO (Railway Transport Officer) told me there was a train from there to Reading at 12.55. It got me there at 2.30 am on the Friday morning, and I felt awful. I was ill all that day. Daphne came on the Saturday with a weekend pass, but I was too bad to leave home. The date was 6 June 1944 – 'D-Day', when the Allied troops landed in France. For me, it was 'diarrhoea day' and I was admitted to an isolation room in the Sick Quarters of the local RAF unit. It was feared I had typhoid. The liver was not to blame. It was all due to the stagnant, green, smelly, rat-infested water. My parents visited me every day and Daphne came again at the next weekend. I was cleared to return to Hixon on 13 June, when I had to report 'sick' (to say I was well!). I was still weak from dehydration and lack of food, and I was excused from flying for another week. During that time, the rest of the crew practised circuits and landings (roundabouts and ricochets). The Derby was run on 17 June so Daphne backed a horse called 'Happy Landings' which came third. She also drew a horse in her office sweepstake (Tehran) which came second, so she did well. On 24 June, I proposed to her by letter and we became engaged. (It was nothing to do with her sudden wealth!)

From 24 June to 4 July our crew did several long night-flights including cross-countries and practice bombing, and, one night we went on a 'Bullseye' excursion over the North Sea to support operational aircraft by deceiving the Germans into thinking a bombing force was on its way to some other target.

We were then given seven days' leave and I went to Gloucester, where Daphne's landlady let me sleep in a caravan in her garden. Having at last got engaged, we looked at rings in Gloucester and Cheltenham where we decided on a fine blue/green zircon flanked by two sparkling diamonds.

My leave ended on 14 July, and the whole crew was ordered to report to Boston Park Camp near Lindholme, about twelve miles from Doncaster. It was another holding unit and once again we were merely passing away time. However, there were a few interesting occurrences, including my journey getting there, which I will include in the next chapter. Let me just say, it was a miserably desolate spot, and we did not fly again for another month.

In conclusion, 'D-Day', or diarrhoea day, had a sad memory for me. My cousin in the Canadian army was preparing to take part in the invasion when his best friend accidentally shot him dead while cleaning their rifles. He is buried, with hundreds of others, in the Canadian Section of Brookwood Military Cemetery, near Woking.

CHAPTER TWENTY-TWO

No Room at the Inn

Travelling in wartime was usually problematic. Often, trains were late or were cancelled, and those actually running were frequently so crowded that it was a job to get on board. I set off on 14 July 1944 to make my way to my new posting to Boston Park Camp, near Doncaster. I arrived at Kings Cross at 9.15 pm to catch the 10.30 train. It was already there, waiting, but it was packed. I walked the length of the platform looking for a doorway which did not have bodies pressed up against it. There wasn't one. I had all my kit with me so I knew I had no hope of getting on board. I was in despair, and retraced my steps. At last, I spotted some lads I had been with at Hixon. They were tightly packed in a luggage van, but they managed to pull me in. I was able to lay my kitbag across a pram and curl my body round a bicycle. Movement was impossible, and, about three hours later I got off at Doncaster, stiff, dirty and with cycle grease all over my uniform.

I waited at Doncaster with the other lads from 2 am until 8 am, weary and dishevelled until a lorry was sent out to pick us up. We were driven about eight miles on a main road before turning on to a lesser one, and eventually on to a country lane. The camp was at the end of the lane. This was Boston Park, Lindholme.

The area was flat and completely desolate; a perfect example of fenland. There was not a house, barn or building of any sort for miles.

We were given breakfast and assigned to a Nissen hut which we shared with another crew. The navigator of the other crew was a good friend of mine called 'Nick' who had trained with me in Canada.

After filling in various forms, we were told that they weren't ready for us and we could go at once on a thirty-six hour leave. I put in for a pass to Birmingham, but then realized that we were too far away from civilisation for me to get there before it would be time to return – and possibly not until after the expiry of my pass. Besides, the rest of the crew were staying on the camp, so I stayed too. We began by familiarizing ourselves with the layout of the camp and getting to know the other crews.

The main camp was about two miles away, comprising the airfield, a camp post office, a cinema, and a small YMCA. Here, we could get tea or beer, but no razor blades, soap, shaving cream or boot or button polish. And no barber for eleven miles. There were a few baths, but to use them we had to get a chit from the adjutant the day before. However, behind the Mess, we found half a dozen showers – not very clean and with no temperature controls. 'Better'n nowt' I was told.

After lunch, we set off for Doncaster. We had to walk about four miles to the main road where we were able to catch a bus. This was fortunate as we were weary from our uncomfortable, overnight travelling. We split up into groups, and Ron Hales and I found a café where we got beans and chips. Two middle-aged ladies sat opposite us and Ron soon struck up a conversation with them. Impromptu chit-chat and comic observations were a strong point with Ron and he kept the ladies amused. As a result, they shared with us the strawberries and cherries they were eating.

We then went to a cinema and found a place where we could get a fish and chips supper. Over the meal, we discussed how we were going to get back to camp. A chap in the café told us there was a bus for war-workers going most of the way, but airmen were not allowed on it. However, he said it was not usually full and, as he knew the driver, he would see if he would take us. All was well, and they dropped us about four miles from the camp site. The rest of our crew had managed to return before us, and we all slept soundly that night.

The following day, we again split into small groups and, this time, I paired up with Max Leversha, our Australian wireless operator. We walked along the deserted country lanes until at last we met a farm worker who told us there was a pub about a mile ahead. That meant it was about six miles from the camp, and when we reached it, it was closed, with a 'NO SUPPLIES' sign on the door. Max and I did not drink beer so a soft drink would have been welcome after our long walk. We reckoned the pub would probably have soft drinks in stock but we couldn't raise the landlord. The pub was at a road junction and as we were waiting a bus came along. We spoke to the driver who told us there was another pub about three miles further along his route so we got aboard and got our soft drinks there. We asked about a bus back towards camp but there wasn't one due for another two hours, so we walked. We reckoned that we had walked about sixteen miles that day. Once again, we slept well.

At the end of our thirty-six hour leave, we were left just hanging about. The officers did gardening and the NCOs did various odd jobs, and acted as duty crew on the aerodrome, and main camp. This included supervising the ablutions, the stores, the boiler rooms, and looking after new arrivals. At night, two members of the duty crew were assigned to the Station Office to answer phones and deal with security, and the wireless operator had to attend to the beacons on the airfield.

In a matter of days, we all had colds, and Peter, our rear gunner, was so poorly that he had to go into the sick bay. The bedding issued to us was damp, and although it was summer, the low fenland was shrouded in mist overnight.

On our turn for night duty, Ray Forbes, our Australian bomb aimer and I, manned the office. The typewriter came in handy to type letters to Daphne and my parents. We had an electric kettle and some tea and we were told that milk would be left for us. It was, but it must have been left several days earlier – it was curdled and sour. Ray had had a food parcel from Australia and he produced some oxtail soup – and that had gone 'off'. But we were so cold, we needed something to warm ourselves so we heated it, drank it, and survived.

The following night, George, our pilot, went drinking in the bar in the main camp, with 'Nick' the other navigator sharing our hut. They returned quite late after the rest of us had gone to bed. They were quite 'merry' and woke us up. Then, after changing into pyjamas, they left and began circling the parade square outside the hut on a bicycle – George pedalling with 'Nick' on the crossbar! Progress, understandably, was very erratic and, after a deal of wobbling, they both fell off. The rest of us picked them up and put them to bed. Surprisingly, they did not appear to be hurt – probably because they were used to doing 'circuits and bumps'!

The next night, George went out on the beer again. He staggered back into the hut and was promptly sick. He lay on his bed crying 'Never again!' And he wasn't the only one. Ray Forbes had returned a little before George with his hand wrapped in a cloth. During his drinking session, someone had bet him that he couldn't punch a hole in a wooden door. The drink told Ray that he could, but the door won!

As a non-drinker, I was getting worried about my future with this crew. Max, the wireless operator didn't drink, so that was all right, and Peter seemed only to get happy on his booze. But I had seen George, Ray and Ron all severely squiffy. I hoped they were not going to do so once we had started flying again. I put it down to being their way of over-coming the frustration of so much time-wasting and hanging about.

Fortunately, we were going to move on in a few days. Before that, we were given a weekend leave. I phoned Daphne to meet me at Birmingham Station, but because of the remoteness of my camp and the unreliable trains, I did not arrive there until late. We were unable to get accommodation at a YMCA or a Forces Hostel but I was not worried as I knew of several hotels in the Hagley Road. We set off in the twilight but not one hotel would take us – all claiming to be full. Eventually, we reached the end of the very long Hagley Road on the outskirts of the city and the beginning of woodland.

It was, by then, quite dark and we were tired and dispirited. A few minuets after midnight, we arrived at number 405, Hagley Road. It was a large house which looked as if it might be a private hotel, and lights were visible around the edges of the blackout material. We rang the bell, and a man aged about fifty came to the door. We told him we were looking for somewhere to stay and that we had walked all the way from the city centre, and he told us that it was his private house. He thought there were no more hotels further on, but wished us luck. We moved on, but there were only a few more houses before the end of the road. Daphne began to cry, and all I could suggest was that we retraced our steps in the hope of finding a side turning with hotels.

As we turned back, we met the gentleman from the house we had just left. He told us that we would never find anywhere to stay at that time of night. He had spoken with his wife and they had agreed that we could spend the night with them. He said they had a son and daughter in the Forces, and if they ever found themselves in the position we were in, they hoped someone would be sympathetic to them.

We went back to the house and the lady asked if we were married. When we told her we were only engaged, she said 'Never mind, I'll make up a bed in the attic'. She made us some hot cocoa which was most welcome and then showed Daphne to her room on the first floor and me to my room in the attic. When I unpacked my haversack, I found that an OXO cube, which I carried for emergencies, had been melted by the heat in the train, and my pyjama trousers were messed up by the sticky brown substance. I could hardly get into that bed with them like that, so I had to go trouserless and hope that there would be no air raid or other need for me to have to get up in the night.

In the morning, the lady laid a table and served us a marvellous break-fast of bacon, toast and strawberry jam. We were overwhelmed by their kindness, but they would not accept any money from us. Many years later, I called at the house, not expecting to find them still alive, but I thought perhaps one of their children might be there, and I could express my thanks to them. The house had been converted into multiple flats.

The sympathetic reception given to us stays in our minds. On my return to camp the next day, the crew was immediately posted to Blyton, near Gainsborough.

CHAPTER TWENTY-THREE

Per Ardua
Ad-Renalin

We arrived at Blyton on Tuesday 25 July 1944 but there was nothing for us to do until Wednesday 2 August. Our leave on 22/23 July could easily have been extended. The futility of keeping aircrew on holding units or training stations where they were either wasting their time on chores, or receiving no training whatsoever, was frustrating and demoralizing. It was senseless and it occurred all too often.

The official title of the Blyton unit was No. 1662 CU (Conversion Unit) where crews were acclimatized to fly in four-engined aircraft. In our case, they were Halifax Twos. It was here that our crew was made up to its full strength of seven by the addition of a flight engineer. This was Ray Clarke ('Nobby'), a young lad from Leicester.

During our first week, when we were idle, George was, once more, having too much to drink and I kept nagging him about it. Once he began flying the Halifaxes he had plenty to concentrate on and he moderated his intake of liquor. He was commissioned within a few days as a Pilot Officer but he could not get away to buy his uniform, so he stayed with us as an NCO. This was a good thing, as it kept us all together as a 'family'. Once George was separated from us by living and eating in officers' quarters, it was not the same, and not good for the crew.

As the navigator, I was attending training courses for some days after the others, who all flew with George and a 'screen' pilot (a qualified instructor) doing circuits and bumps. I went with them only once when the screen pilot had judged George ready to go solo. George put the plane down with a heck of a thump and we ballooned up, bounced again and, with Nobby's help with the throttles, climbed away to make a second attempt. Perfectly.

My training included learning how to use a new navigation device known as H2S that, from a housing under the belly of the aircraft, sent a radar beam down to the ground. The beam rebounded to the aircraft and was transferred to a monitor screen on the navigator's table showing an outline of coasts, rivers and built-up areas.

After one or two cross-country navigation flights we went on another 'Bullseye' (spoof raid). We were one of 182 training aircraft in a mainstream 'diversion support' exercise over the North Sea, while the main force was attacking Darmstadt and Russelsheim in central Germany. We took off at 10 pm and landed without incident at 3 am on 26 August. It was our first experience of being in a large force of four-engined bombers, all packed closely together, and it was a wonderful sight. There were no thrills as regards enemy aircraft, but the excitement was there and the adrenalin was flowing. By 4 pm the same afternoon, after a brief sleep, we were up again on a cross-country, which meant, as navigator, I was busy as charts had to be prepared and navigation and meteorological briefings attended.

There was always much to be done by navigators before a flight, and when that work was wasted by the trip being 'scrubbed' (cancelled), it was inevitable that the navigators felt hard done by. On two successive nights, we had three different briefings, due to bad weather, and on both nights we had gone out to the aircraft before the flights were cancelled. On the second occasion, we had to walk back some distance to our cold Nissen hut in pouring rain which soaked right through to our underclothes. We had dim lights in the hut, but plenty of running water – through the roof and under the door! We got a small fire going and managed to dry some of our clothing. Some of the other crews were not so lucky. Fuel for the fires was not readily available – in fact it was very scarce. We had managed to filch some in the darkness. Our wireless operator, Max, was celebrating (if that's what you can call it) his 20th birthday, and he had had a food parcel from Australia, so we sat around the fire in various states of undress while our garments steamed in front of us, eating oxtail soup, peaches and cream, and home-made birthday cake, followed by warmed up Horlicks. After that we played cards until at last going to bed. The fire had burned itself out.

We had bad weather for several days and nights and, on one such night, Ray, 'Nobby', Ron and Peter went out in the rain and the darkness to go drinking. On the way back, they saw a small white rabbit run across the path and into the open doorway of a hut. Peter rushed after it and went to switch on the light. Peter was wet and the light switch was faulty; he couldn't let go of it. Ray managed to release him, but the forces of the current split Peter's finger badly. He came back to our hut with a handkerchief round his very gory finger, but proudly nursing the rabbit. He had to get his finger properly dressed in the morning, and was unable to fly for some days.

The rabbit was a tame one and we kept it in a wire cage in the locker room where we kept our flying kit. It was quite happy there, and we managed to get lettuce for it in the Mess. We also gave it clover and grass. Each day, I gave it water and cleaned it out – Peter being in sick quarters with a cold as well as his torn finger.

We all had colds, and Ron joined Peter in the sick bay. The rest of us did not go sick. Instead, we were given leave, and George went home to get his uniform. I went to Reading and had the usual prolonged journey back. I left Reading at midday on the Sunday to catch a train from Kings Cross to Retford with a wait there till 4 am for the train to Gainsborough, arriving an hour later, with a six mile walk to the camp. George returned looking spick-and-span in his new Pilot Officer's uniform, and driving his own car – a Lanchester.

We were then told we were not wanted till the Thursday. If only we had known, we could have had a longer leave. There was no point in going far, so I slipped across to Harrogate to see my brother who, by then, was working there in the Ministry of Aircraft Production. I arrived at 8 pm and had a meal at the YMCA before visiting my brother, and then returning to the YMCA for the night. I saw my brother again the next day but it rained incessantly so we could not do anything and I went back to camp late that night. Peter was still in the sick bay and Ray Forbes was down with a bad sore throat. Our living conditions were awful.

We had only to do a high level bombing practice to finish our course but the weather held us up. At last we got away and did a dummy run to level the bomb sight and check the instruments. That done, we called up the bombing range on the R/T (radio telephone) to get permission to start. The radio was dead! We returned to base, and got the radio repaired and prepared to take off again. On running up the engines, one rapidly developed a high temperature. We had to let it cool down and let the ground crew work on it. George and 'Nobby' went aboard and tested it, and all was well. The rest if us began climbing in, when Ray Forbes noticed that a tyre was looking soft. The ground crew reported a faulty valve. We went back to the Flight Office and asked for another aircraft. One was found, and we trudged off to its dispersal point. After all the usual checks, we taxied towards the runway. As we lined up for take-off, Flying Control called us up on the radio 'Your detail is cancelled owing to weather conditions. Return to dispersal'. We said some harsh words as we were all pretty disgruntled. As we wearily made our way back to the Flight Office, Ray, in his customary, sardonic way, remarked – 'I say, George, next time they give us an aircraft would you mind asking the CO to get someone with just a little engineering knowledge to go and give it the once-over just a casual glance, you know – he needn't be too ambitious about it so long as he recognizes it as an aeroplane and makes sure it has wheels on!'

We never did that bombing run. They told us we were not going to be flying Halifaxes after all, but Lancasters. So we were posted to No. 1 LFS (Lancaster Flying School) at Hemswell. We left the rabbit in the care of the corporal in charge of the parachute section.

Hemswell was a pre-war station and (joy of joys) we were housed in brick-built huts. They were warmer and dry. We attended lectures and studied for a week, and then we flew for only two days – once on 16 September and three times on the 17th. One trip was for fighter affiliation, to allow George to master the technique of weaving and diving (corkscrewing) to escape from a fighter, and then the gunners were given the opportunity of lining up their guns on a moving 'enemy' target.

We stayed at Hemswell for only ten days before moving on to our permanent operational squadron (No. 166) at Kirmington, near Grimsby on 19 September.

A Bastard Kangaroo

We took up duty at No. 166 Squadron, Kirmington on 20 September 1944. After the war it became Humberside Airport, but in 1944, although the aerodrome was no worse than any other airfield, the rest of the buildings were detestable. The NCO's Nissen huts were set in a wood alongside the grand estate of Brocklesby Park, a good mile from the aerodrome, with the Sergeant's Mess midway between the two. The officers lived much nearer the airfield, in brick-built huts.

After being at a permanent RAF station at Hemswell, it came as something of a shock to be back in cold, damp Nissen huts. We had expected something better for our operational squadron base where (hopefully) we would be staying for several months. The conditions were far from ideal for the morale of aircrews under the strains of incessant calls to briefings, planning routes and plotting charts, and ultimately 'dicing with death' as operational sorties were called. In my first letter to Daphne after arriving at the base, I wrote – 'My first impression of Kirmington is very poor. In fact, to think that it is to be our permanent home from now on, makes me shudder'.

Nor was our reception very uplifting. We received a brief talk about the facilities on the station, and the location of the main buildings with which we would be concerned, and our crew was then assigned to 'A' Flight.

Because of the dispersed layout of the station, crews were issued with bikes, but none was available at first. When we got ours, all were in a poor state, with flat tyres and other problems. Fortunately, Max, our wireless operator was able to borrow a repair outfit from a maintenance crew servicing an aircraft's wheels. I was hoping that the squadron's planes were in better shape than their bikes. I mended about six punctures, fitted new valves, bashed the forks into roughly the right positions, and patched up and tightened the saddles. All the brakes were faulty and needed adjustments. No one in the bike store seemed bothered about the condition of the bikes – after all, they were only for the aircrews, and, most probably, the bikes would be passed on to some other 'bods' in a day or two!

After looking at our sparse acquaintance with Lancasters, the Flight Commander – a serious but pleasant squadron leader – decided to send us on two or three training flights before becoming operational.

On 23 September we went on an early morning cross-country flight of four hours, and on the night of the 26th we combined a practice bombing exercise at Alkborough, with a cross-country navigation flight until 4 am. Finally, on the 2 October, we gave the air gunners experience of firing from their newly-fitted 0.5 inch Browning machine guns, and gun turret manipulation out at sea off Mablethorpe.

On returning from this flight, there was a panic stricken shout of 'Get down, you bastard!' from George, our pilot, as he misjudged his landing approach and caused the plane to bounce about 50 feet. She settled down after a few more hops, but Ron, the mid-upper gunner suffered a cut eye and Peter in the rear turret was bruised. I clung on to the edges of my navigation table – and hoped that someone up above was watching over us.

During these first few days on the squadron, George had adopted a somewhat officious and bossy manner towards the rest of us, no doubt feeling his feet as a new officer and captain of his aircraft. It was at about this time that the 'cruse' incident occurred (See Chapter 20). On this occasion, it was again Ray Forbes, our Australian bomb aimer, who put George in his place by dryly asking if he was trying to mate with a kangaroo!

CHAPTER TWENTY-FIVE

Initiation to Ops

Having now joined our operational squadron, we know that our peaceful practice flights were no more. Indeed, the perils of operational flying were brought home to us on the day of our very first training flight on the squadron, 23 September 1944.

The pleasant Flight Commander who had welcomed us a few days earlier took off with his crew at 18.30 hours to bomb the docks and industrial area of Neuss, on the Rhine near Dusseldorf. He did not return and nor did two other aircraft. In fact, the Flight Commander had survived, but we did not hear of the details until much later. It appeared that as he did his bombing run, a Ju 88 attacked, killing the rear gunner who, before he died managed to destroy it. The navigator was severely wounded, and the hydraulic system was wrecked so that the gun turrets could not be turned or the bomb doors opened. One engine was out of action. The pilot ordered the bomb aimer to release the bombs, and their weight burst open the doors and the bombs fell away. But the doors could not be closed and the wind whistled up through the fuselage, as the pilot turned for home. The navigator was in a poor shape and losing blood. He was bitterly cold and all his navigation equipment was out of action. He still managed to guide his pilot back to the English coast and to the emergency landing ground at Manston, near Dover. The pilot made a crash landing without injuring the crew, but the plane was a write-off. He was awarded the Distinguished Service Order (DSO) and the navigator received the NCO equivalent, the Conspicuous Gallantry Medal (CGM-Flying). There they were, two brave men, flying together, and each skilful at their jobs, but, just as officers lived on brick-built huts and NCOs lived in Nissen huts, the archaic class distinction required them to be honoured differently.

Of the other two aircraft that were lost, nothing was ever heard of one aircraft or of its crew, while some crew members of the other aircraft, which had been shot down, were taken prisoner, including the navigator who had already been shot down earlier in the year. Then, he had evaded capture and had returned to England only a few days before being shot down again.

So, on the day of our first flight, three aircraft had been lost. Perhaps that was how it was that we were suddenly issued with bikes. Such was our initiation.

On four successive days from 25 September the squadron made daylight attacks on the Calais area. Heavy cloud presented difficulties, but the raids were sufficient to cause the Germans to surrender to the advancing Canadian troops. By this time, the Allies controlled all the Channel ports except Dunkirk which was still in German hands and was heavily defended. However, the Allied ground forces could make only slow progress as communication routes and facilities inland were so badly damaged.

German troops were also entrenched in the area from Antwerp along the River Scheldt through to the Dutch island of Walcheren, on which was the town of Flushing. The island was made up of reclaimed low-lying land (known as 'polder') below sea level and protected by sea walls. On 3 October the squadron bombed the sea walls at Westkapelle at the western end of the island, so that the North Sea flooded the important section where enemy gun emplacements were dominating the approaches to the port of Antwerp. Other guns were still operating, but the main threat to the Allied forces had been destroyed.

Our crew had been standing by to make this our first bombing raid, but we were not needed, and the next day, 4 October we were un-expectedly sent on leave until early morning on Saturday, 7 October. I travelled to Gloucester to be with Daphne on the Thursday, and went to my parents' home at Reading on Friday morning. I had to leave them at 7 pm and although it was pouring with rain, and a fierce wind blowing, my mother insisted in coming out in the dark, and seeing me off at the station.

I had not told my parents that I was now on an operational bombing station, but I expect my mother suspected it, and was fearful for me, having lost brothers in the First World War. Also, night after night, Reading was the assembly point for the main bomber force and she was used to seeing Halifaxes and Lancasters circling overhead.

As we crossed the road to the bus stop, my mother's hat blew off and went rolling down the hill. I rushed off and recovered it but my mother had followed and been bowled over by the force of the wind. I found her in a heap on the wet pavement. She had cut her nose and her leg. I picked her up and took her home, but as my bus was due, I had to leave her with my father. I missed the bus, but the next one got me to the station just in time, and I travelled through the night to be back in Kirmington by 7.15 on Saturday morning.

While we were on leave, the squadron had sent thirty aircraft to attack Saarbrucken on 5 October to assist the American army by cutting the railway supply lines to the German troops. A Ju 88 attacked one plane and a Focke Wolfe 190 attacked another, but both our planes came through safely, although on return, nineteen crews were diverted to other aerodromes because of the fog which continually caused problems at Kirmington.

When I got back to my hut at 7.15 am that Saturday morning, the rest of the crew went off to breakfast while I stayed to clean my greatcoat which was stained with my mother's blood. When I joined them, they told me we had to go straight away for a briefing for a morning operation. After the briefing, we returned to the Mess to snatch a quick breakfast, then back to the navigation office to draw up charts and flight plans for take-off at 11.45 am.

We had been travelling all night without sleep, and now we were being sent on our very first bombing mission. What a way to begin. Thankfully, it was to be a daylight raid for these were less testing than flying in the dark.

We were to destroy road and rail communications at Emmerich on the Rhine, near Arnhem on the Holland/German border. We flew a very direct route from Mablethorpe across the North Sea to the Dutch coast, north of the Hague and on to the target for about ninety miles. After bombing, we turned south-west for seventy miles and then westwards towards Ostende and back to base. The weather there was atrocious, but we managed to get down safely, while seventeen planes had to be diverted to Hemswell. For us, it was a straightforward flight of four and a half hours, but three Lancasters were lost, one being from our squadron, and two others were severely damaged. The crew shot down were on only their third operation. Inexperienced crews were often early casualties; probably because they were timed to bomb towards the end of an attack, after the experienced teams had, normally, identified the target for the benefit of the latecomers. By that time, the ground defences were ready for the raiders, and fighter planes likely to have arrived.

Our second operation was on 11 October. It was another daylight raid, this time to destroy gun batteries at Fort Frederick Hendrik at Breskens, on the south bank of the River Scheldt. This was a few miles south of the island of Walcheren, which had already been flooded by the raid on 3 October.

We were one of only thirteen aircraft on the raid, but being newcomers, we were timed to bomb near the end of the attack. By that time, there was so much smoke and dust from those bombing before us, that the Master Bomber called off the rest of the mission. Our trip was recorded as 'abortive', but as we had reached the target and had been kept circling while waiting for instructions – never a pleasant experience – it was deemed that it should count as an operational flight towards our tour of duty. A tour consisted, at that time, of thirty ops. It was a beautiful sunny afternoon and as we circled over Walcheren Island awaiting instructions, we could see the completely submerged houses and other buildings below – a really fantastic sight.

The following day, the squadron sent only eight planes to finish the raid, destroying two gun emplacements and damaging another two. Our presence was not required.

There were no losses from these two raids, but on the second day a squadron plane on fighter affiliation training collided with the Hurricane 'attacking' it, and both planes crashed near Hemswell airfield. The Hurricane pilot and ten crew in the Lancaster were killed. There was the usual mist and heavy cloud, so perhaps when the Lancaster went into a 'corkscrew', poor visibility caused the disaster.

At this time, I was dosing myself with aspirin, Zube cough sweets and menthol inhalant to fight off a bad cold. The terribly damp, foggy conditions and the unheated huts resulted in crews being repeatedly unfit to fly, and often they flew when far from well.

CHAPTER TWENTY-SIX

Eau Dear Cologne

Until September 1944, RAF Bomber Command had been under the direct control of General Eisenhower, but then Air Marshal 'Bomber' Harris regained control. Under Eisenhower the heavy bombers had been largely engaged on supporting the Allied forces in France, Holland and Belgium. The Harris plan was to concentrate attacks on Germany's industries, oil and communications. He christened his plan 'Hurricane' and as a result, half of the total weight of bombs dropped on German targets was delivered between August 1944 and May 1945. These bombs were also much more powerful due to the introduction of aluminised explosives.

As a result of the new campaign, the squadron launched two attacks on Duisburg in the Ruhr (known to the aircrews as 'Happy Valley') where the defences were fearsome. The first raid took place early in the morning of 14 October and the second was launched late that same night. Over a thousand planes were used on each attack. One squadron plane was lost on each raid. The following night, the squadron sent a small force to bomb the major naval base at Wilhelmshaven. It was a successful raid and no further attacks on that base were necessary. More importantly, all our aircraft returned safely.

Our crew did not take part in those three raids and as we were not being used, we went on seven days' leave from Tuesday 17 October until Monday the 23rd. I sent a telegram to Daphne and we both stayed at her home as my parents were taking their first holiday since the outbreak of war, at Lyme Regis.

Our leave was probably due to the build up of strength at Kirmington, and on 7 October, it was announced that twenty-seven crews would become the re-formed 153 Squadron. They remained with us until the middle of the month, when they were transferred to Scampton, near Lincoln. We lost several of our mates, particularly in my case, Freddy Fish and 'Gus' Cole who had trained with me in Canada. Freddy organized the 153 Squadron reunions after the war, and remained a good friend of mine until his death in May 2004 on the morning after his squadron reunion. Poor 'Gus' did not survive for long after leaving Kirmington.

I met Freddy on Kings Cross station as I made my way back to Kirmington on 23 October; he had to change at Grantham, and I went on to Retford where I was lucky to find that the last train to Barnetby (the nearest station to Kirmington) had been delayed, and was waiting. When going on leave, we used to cycle to Barnetby and leave our bikes there, collecting them on our return. Ron and Peter, my two air gunners were on the same train and we all cycled back to the airfield together.

While we were on leave, the squadron made a raid on Stuttgart without incurring any losses, but during the preparations an incendiary bomb exploded in the bomb store and killed a young airman.

On Monday the 23rd, while were returning from leave, nineteen squadron planes took part in a one thousand bomber raid on Essen. One of our planes was struck by a bomb dropped from another aircraft above it. The bomb tore through one wing and cut the fuel line to one engine, but the pilot was able to keep the machine under control and make an emergency landing at Manston. This sort of incident was not uncommon, but usually resulted in the lower aircraft crashing out of control. We saw two or three accidents like it during our tour, and on one occasion it very nearly happened to ourselves.

We bombed the Krupps armaments works at Essen as our third 'op' in a daylight raid on Wednesday, 25 October, with all our planes returning. The following day, six crews went on a minelaying trip – nicknamed 'gardening' – off Heligoland. This was always a dangerous experience because of the heavy coastal defences. One crew on their nineteenth 'op' failed to return.

We did our fourth 'op' on 28 October. It was a daylight raid on Cologne. There were separate raids on two areas of the city, Mulheim in the north-east, and Zollstuck in the south-west. Both areas were severely devastated at a cost of four Halifaxes and three Lancasters, but all twenty-two from Kirmington came through.

On Sunday 29 October, the squadron attacked some gun positions still operating in the sunken island of Walcheren without loss.

Cologne was attacked again on the 30th. I think it was at this briefing that the Navigation Leader observed that many of our mothers were acquainted with Eau de Cologne, but would navigators please note that Cologne was not on the Oder – a river well to the east, near the Polish border – but on the Rhine.

Twenty-five squadron planes took off just after 5 pm for a six and a half hour operation. It was our fifth and all the crews got home. On this raid, the attacks were directed at the Braunsfield, Lindenthal. Klettenberg, and Sulz areas of the city.

A repeat attack was made on the 31 October, using a different route, taking an hour less. This time the target was the southern section of Bayental and Zullstock. Normally, we flew at about 16,000 feet on the outward legs of the route but to avoid detection by German radar, we left Reading at less than 3,000 feet until reaching the French coast. This was at the mouth of the Somme, opposite Eastbourne. We climbed as we flew east towards Liege and then east-north-east past Bonn and northward to Cologne. As we approached, a ring of searchlights sprang up and ahead heavy flak was bursting below us from the anti-aircraft guns defending the Ruhr. The bursts became closer, and a Lancaster alongside us exploded and disappeared. Others were dodging to avoid the search-lights, and our two gunners were continually shouting out warnings to George to dive or turn – not to escape from fighters as was the norm – but to avoid 'friendly' aircraft who were weaving around us to escape the many probing beams. Eventually a searchlight settled on us and the inside of the aircraft was momentarily lit up as George 'corkscrewed'. Most of the flak was bursting below us, and lifting us as it 'bumped'. But with the dive of the corkscrew, we were down amongst it. And the searchlight operators were not in a hurry to let us get away. It was George's first experience of evading a cone of searchlights and it seemed ages before we slipped back into darkness. It was probably only about 20 seconds.

During the spiralling dive, the 'G' force was such that movement was difficult and it was impossible not to feel fear. All moveable items on my navigation table leapt upwards and disappeared.

Despite the flak and the searchlights all our aircraft returned, and only two were lost out of a force of about five hundred. However, one of our crews had an exciting time avoiding attacks by two Ju 88s. They shot one down, but the other pressed on with the attack. The Lancaster dived down through the cloud below, reaching such a speed that the pilot had to be helped to pull back the control column. Not only did they pull out of the dive, they shot back up through the cloud and, by good fortune, came out right beneath the enemy fighter. It was a sitting duck, and they destroyed that one too.

Squadron aircraft were identified by a letter of the alphabet and the phonetic name for that letter. On this trip, we flew in 'I – ITEM' and this became 'our' kite which we flew on most of our future sorties.

Since our arrival on the squadron, we had completed six operations and eight planes had been lost. All my navigation charts and logs had been collected after each flight and scrutinized by the Navigation Leader, and then sent to Bomber Command for checking. Apparently, they were satisfactory and I was never called to account for any faults.

All charts and logs were completed in pencil. The changes in air pressure soon taught crews never to carry fountain pens. Pencils in wartime were described as 'utility' with soft leads which blurred easily when rubbed. Daphne managed to get me some scarce hard-leaded ones which were much better. She had my name put on them, which amused Ray Forbes, our bomb aimer, who used to come back to do a spot of navigation beside me on homeward legs, to keep his eye in. Until, then, he was always pinching my pencils!

CHAPTER TWENTY-SEVEN

Going Through the Roof

Having been allocated our own aircraft – 'I–ITEM' we spent much of our time getting to know our ground crew who worked on it in its dispersal (parking) bay. This bay was at the furthest part of the airfield from the main entrance, the offices, and the control tower. One other aircraft was parked near us – 'E–EASY', which we had already flown in once. It was an isolated spot beside a low boundary hedge, beyond which, was a short road containing about half a dozen farm workers' houses.

A hole had mysteriously appeared in the hedge, and one of the ground crew used to go through it to get to the house of a Mr and Mrs Stanley, with whom he was billeted. The Stanleys were a young couple with two small children, and we all went through the hole to meet them. The Stanleys were pig farmers, and Mrs Stanley used to feed us with delicious home-made pork pies. She would also bring out hot tea if we were standing around on a cold night waiting for take-off, or in the daytime, when the airfield was fogbound. At that time, the squadron had no thermos flasks for us to take on our sorties. We also took our bikes through the hole as a short cut to the road leading to Barnetby Station when going on leave.

We took a pride in 'ITEM' as well as particular care of the parts of her which concerned us most.

Our pilot, George Lee, was short and plumpish and had been a car salesman in 'civvy' street. He was about thirty, some ten years older than most of us, and, although he was a fine pilot, he was curiously indecisive at times. He habitually sought my advice as decision maker when we were in the air. 'What shall we do, Fizz?' was a frequent cry. Also, when we were being attacked by fighters the gunners would urgently order him to 'corkscrew' and he would delay, shouting 'Which way?' In unison we would all shout back – 'Any bloody way!' Having got his commission,

Don Feesey with his
older brother at
Seaford during 1938.

The author by the River Thames at Reading in 1942.

In the Air Training Corps in 1941.

Don when an Aircrew Trainee – AC2 – in 1942

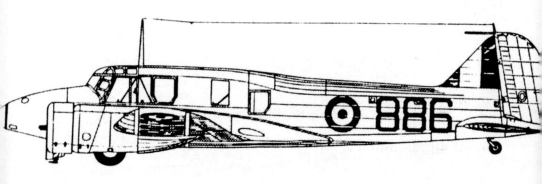

An Avro Anson.

The author shopping in Edmonton, Canada.

Navigation Course 80 N.1. *Left to right – Back row:* Dobson, Cole, Edmond, Feesey. Haynes. *Middle Row:* Cooper, Robinson, Macleod, Fish, Smith, Lovell, Farrand, Morrison, Toogood, Fry, Anderson, Marsh. *Front Row:* Tate, Baker, Nichols, F/Lt. Jones, F/Lt. Nash, Seaward, Simpson, Eccleston.

'Fizz' with his brother Peter and Ron Hales at Birk Crag, Harrogate in 1944...

...and with his wife, Daphne, at the same spot in 1991.

The crew of AS'I' (Item) – *Invinsible Isles*. No. 166 Squadron 1945. *Left to right:* Ray Forbes (Bomb Aimer), Ray 'Nobby' Clarke (Flight Engineer), Peter Turley (Rear Gunner), George Lee (Pilot), Don 'Fizz' Feesey (Navigator), Ron Hales (Mid Upper Gunner) and Max Leversha (Wireless Operator).

The navigation team – 'Fizz' and Forbes.

Ray Forbes (with no head for heights!) and Max Leversha. 'Fizz', 'Nobby' and Ron Hales with Peter Turley in his turret. (When the pilot ordered Peter to bale out – did he have him over a barrel or two?)

Our ground crew – to whom we owed so much.

Flight Engineer 'Nobby' Clarke in the cockpit of 'ITEM' – *Invinsible Isles*.

The crew.

'Fizz' and his
Fiancée –
Rhapsody in
Blue!

Lost in the Alps.

'Dusty" Miller's grave in Rheinberg War Cemetery, Germany.

JANUARY 26, 1945

DEATH FLIGHT OF A ME 410

Destroyed By Meopham Air Gunner

A ME 410 swooped down on the Lancaster bomber "O for Orange" as it was approaching Nuremberg recently and opened fire.

The Lancaster's bomb-aimer was wounded in the leg.

The mid-upper gunner Sergt. R. A. Hales, youngest son of Mrs. Hales, 4, Station Road, Meopham, and the late Mr. E. Hales, returned fire and hit the Messerschmitt, which exploded in the air.

SERGT. HALES

The pilot, Flying Officer G. W. J. W. Thompson, of Saskatoon, Sask., Canada took "O for Orange" on to Nuremberg, and the target was identified in fair weather.

Some damage was done to the Lancaster and the bomb release gear caused trouble.

Most of the bombs were dropped, but some hung up and had to be jettisoned later.

Finally, a generator broke loose from its fittings, some minutes after the return flight began. It immediately caught fire.

The outbreak was dealt with promptly and did not spread.

It was not put out, however, until every extinguisher in the aircraft had been used.

A former pupil at Meopham School, Sergt. Hales is 19 and joined the R.A.F. in October, 1943. He was previously employed at the Rainbow Stores, Gravesend.

Newspaper report about Ron Hales.

Gunsight views of an Me 410.

Crew members under the mid-upper turret.

The White Cliffs of Dover.

At home with Daphne.

Don and Daphne's marriage in 1945.

on Feesey at the end of the war.

Don Feesey, Ron Hales and Peter Turley at the 166 Squadron Memorial in Kirmington Village in 1989.

e memorial plaque.

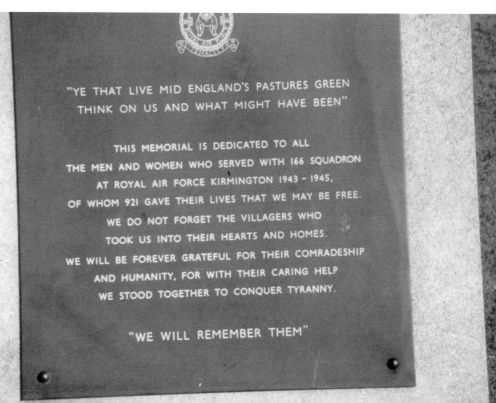

"YE THAT LIVE MID ENGLAND'S PASTURES GREEN
THINK ON US AND WHAT MIGHT HAVE BEEN"

THIS MEMORIAL IS DEDICATED TO ALL
THE MEN AND WOMEN WHO SERVED WITH 166 SQUADRON
AT ROYAL AIR FORCE KIRMINGTON 1943 - 1945,
OF WHOM 921 GAVE THEIR LIVES THAT WE MAY BE FREE.
WE DO NOT FORGET THE VILLAGERS WHO
TOOK US INTO THEIR HEARTS AND HOMES.
WE WILL BE FOREVER GRATEFUL FOR THEIR COMRADESHIP
AND HUMANITY, FOR WITH THEIR CARING HELP
WE STOOD TOGETHER TO CONQUER TYRANNY.

"WE WILL REMEMBER THEM"

"Fizz' and Daphne in 1991.

'Fizz' wearing his Lancaster tie in 1995.

Pilot George Lee with his two year-old son in 1947. (See Appendix)

he sometimes assumed a bossy attitude towards the rest of the crew when on the ground, and he was never without his insignia of an officer – his brown leather gloves. He came from Dewsbury, and his wife, Anne, was expecting their first child.

Ray Clarke, the flight engineer, came from Leicester, and he and Max, were the youngest members of the crew. Ray took his job very seriously and, before take-off, he would carefully make sure that we, as well as 'his' engines were properly ready. He was a pillar of strength for the pilot, and, naturally, to us he was 'Nobby'.

Just as well for we already had another Ray in the crew. This being Ray Forbes, our Australian bomb aimer who had had some navigation training. Ray was in his late twenties and had no time for pomposity or senseless rules. He was outspoken, dry, sardonic, and had no respect for 'authority', he was a fine bridge player, and taught all the crew how to play. We played continually when hanging about waiting for briefings or other duties. It became a standing topic among the other crews who jokingly asserted that we played bridge on the navigators' table when on ops. Some seemed to believe it, but in reality, once in the air we all concentrated solely on the job in hand.

The other 'Aussie' in the crew was Max Leversha, our wireless operator. Like 'Nobby' Clarke, he too, showed great concern for the other crew members and ensured that their intercom, oxygen and parachute storage were always in order. Unlike his fellow Australian, Max was careful not to step out of line, but his naivety sometimes caused him to say something well-meant but tactless, and he could be easily kidded along by practical jokers.

Our mid-upper gunner was Ron Hales who came from Kent. He had a fine sense of humour and an outgoing personality, ready to talk and make friends rapidly. He was prepared to have a 'beef' but not so forcibly or sarcastically as Ray Forbes. He was a tall lad and whether or not this gave the shorter George Lee an inferiority complex I can't say, but George often tended to adopt a superior air towards Ron and at one time christened him 'Mutton-head'! But Ron's good nature saw him through, and he was – and still is – always ready to give a helping hand to anyone in need. A good egg if ever there was one.

That leaves the rear gunner, Peter Turley. Peter had not had the best of childhoods, having been brought up with siblings in a children's home. He could always see the funny side of situations and was a bit of a comic. He could keep us cheerful if things were going badly and I was glad to have him in the tail turret, he had a mischievous nature and could easily get into trouble. He suffered with dry eyes and in later years he became nearly blind.

There was a strong bond between crew members – after all we each depended on the others for our safety, and it was imperative that we all got on. Ron, Peter and I have remained close and we have attended squadron reunions together until 2004 when, sadly, they had to cease, as survivors were becoming fewer. The reunions were usually attended by a fair sprinkling of former aircrew from Australia, Canada, New Zealand and South Africa, and also by relatives of those who flew with the squadron but did not survive. George Lee, 'Nobby' Clarke, Ray Forbes and Max Leversha have all died since the end of the war.

So, having bonded also with our own aircraft, we went on our seventh op on the night of Thursday 2 November 1944 when twenty-eight squadron machines helped to form a force of nearly 1,000 bombers which launched a heavy attack on the northern sector of Dusseldorf on the Rhine, north of Cologne. Dusseldorf was the commercial centre of the Rhine/Ruhr industrial area. Naturally, it was very well defended and although all the squadron's planes got home, eleven Halifaxes and eight Lancasters did not. It was the last major raid on this city.

For us, it was not without incident, however. We left England via Eastbourne and crossed to Abbeville on the mouth of the Somme, just as we had done on our last trip. We then went for a long distance, over Antwerp and on towards Duisburg before turning south-east for Dusseldorf. We bombed through a barrage of flak, and turned south-west to fly a roundabout route back to Abbeville. After the searchlights and the shell bursts this leg was peaceful. There was a bright moon and wonderful visibility. Both gunners were keeping their eyes peeled for enemy fighters. Ray in the front turret was also watching out. Suddenly, he called 'Enemy aircraft ahead and below us . . . circling'. George asked 'Nobby' to look out for it but from his window he could not see below. 'What is it?' George asked Ray, 'and has it seen us?'

'No, it's still turning – a Focke-Wulf 190' reported Ray.

'Keep your eyes on it. Ray. Where is it now?'

'Still turning, George. He hasn't seen us, but turn to port about 30 degrees and I'll be able to line my guns up on it'.

It seemed to take ages and at last Ray was satisfied that we were positioned correctly. He came back on the intercom. 'Hold her steady, George . . . exactly right . . . firing now'.

When the guns were firing, the plane shook a little and the rat-tat-tat could be heard inside. On this occasion we heard nothing. We all waited for the noise of the guns. The silence was shattered by Ray using a word which I shall not print.

George asked him if he was all right. There was no reply. The question was repeated, with anxiety in George's voice. Still there was no response. We began to fear the worst.

George persisted. 'Ray! Ray! Are you there? Are you all right?' There was a long pause and then in a quiet tone, Ray muttered that he was all right.

'Did you get it?' asked George. There was silence.

'Did you get it, Ray?' No reply. 'Ray?'

'No George'.

'Well, where is it now?'

'It's gone, George'.

We flew on and I gave George a new course to put us back on our proper route.

When George was satisfied that the FW 190 really had gone, he wanted to know more.

'Ray, are you there?'

'Yes, George'.

'I want to know what happened, Ray. I held her steady and you said you'd got her lined up. So how did you miss it?'

'I didn't miss, George'.

'Ray, I want to know what happened'. Silence.

'Ray? What went wrong?' There was a long pause.

'Ray?'

'I didn't fire, George'.

'Why not?' Silence again.

'Why not? Why didn't you fire?' Silence again.

'Ray?'

'I left the flamin' safety catch on!'

'Christ! Well, take the damn thing off now in case it comes back'. It didn't and we never got our FW 190.

We got back safely and taxied to our dispersal bay. As we finalized all our checks. Ray's voice came over the intercom uttering the same naughty word as before. George asked what had happened now.

'I've done it again, George. I forgot the safety catch was off and I've let off a few rounds'.

'Have you hit anything?'

'No, George, they'll have gone away over the fields.'

All was quiet, so we went off to debriefing and said nothing about it.

In the morning, we went out to our aircraft as usual and all seemed well. We went through our hole and visited the Stanleys. Mr Stanley was there, which was unusual at that time of the day.

'We got woken up last night' he told us. 'One of your lot put some bullets through our roof'.

Ray had to admit that he was the culprit, and told them the story. Fortunately, the damage was only slight and Mr Stanley was able to make the repairs.

It was a case of friendly fire!

CHAPTER TWENTY-EIGHT

Operational Procedures

Crews were warned to stand-by for operational flying early in the day and, as night ops were the normal pattern, they were called to attend the briefing room in the late afternoon. Station police guarded the door and were posted at intervals around the outside of the briefing hut. Windows were masked. Inside there were rows and rows of collapsible chairs, leading to a raised platform at the far end, with about ten more chairs on it and a table. On the wall at the back of the platform hung a large black curtain.

The crews filed in and took their seats in dimmed lights. When all crews were assembled, in came the leaders of each section – navigation, bombing, signals, gunnery, engineering, meteorology and intelligence. The lights went up, and from the doorway came the call – 'All stand for the CO'.

The Station policeman on the door closed it and retired outside, while the CO took his place on the platform. He gave the order to be seated and usually prefaced his briefing by either telling crews it was to be only a short one, or to be prepared for a lengthy and hazardous trip.

In total silence and apprehension, the crews waited for the black curtain to be drawn aside. Behind it was a complete map extending from Britain to beyond Germany in the east, and well up to Sweden and Finland in the north, and Switzerland and Italy in the south. Red tapes ran across the map to pins at each turning point on the route to the target. Direct routes were never used. There were usually many changes of direction, and short legs and long legs to deceive the enemy as to the final objective.

Crews were told the time of take-off and their times to be over the target. In most cases, a pair of crews would be detailed to bomb one minute after the pair ahead of them. Navigators who failed to bomb within a minute either side of their allotted time had to explain it.

Sometimes there was only half a minute between the timed attacks.

The purpose of the raid was explained to the crews and they were told what their bombing loads were. They were not all the same. Generally, they all carried a 4,000 lb 'cookie', a long cylindrical bomb carried horizontally in the bomb bay under the aircraft, and a mixture of 1,000 lb and 500 lb finned bombs, plus cases of incendiaries. The engineers made notes of the quantity of fuel to be carried in the six tanks in the wings, and the overall weight of the aircraft with bombs, fuel and crew. They had to work out how to gauge the use of the fuel and when to change tanks provided all went well and fuel was not lost if tanks were punctured. The tanks were self-sealing so far as small holes were concerned, but if there should be large ruptures, petrol was blown back over the wings and lost. In most cases it caught fire from the exhaust from the engines. The engineer had to recalculate the remaining quantity and how long it would last.

Pilots and gunners were warned about known anti-aircraft emplacements and searchlight batteries, and wireless operators were briefed on radio channels, etc. The Bombing Leader explained about target markings; usually Pathfinder aircraft would precede the main force guided by 'Oboe' (radio beams which would intersect at a point over the target). The Pathfinders would release coloured flares ('Wanganui sky markers') to indicate aiming points.

The 'Met.' (Meteorology) Officer would paint a general picture of weather conditions along the route and, later, give a detailed briefing to the navigators and bomb aimers. But pilots needed to know about cloud heights and types, and temperatures as icing on wings caused many planes to go out of control.

The CO and the Section leaders departed, apart from the Navigation Leader and the Met. Officer who gave the navigators and bomb aimers detailed briefings, especially about wind speeds and directions. The other crew members left to put on their flying gear and to take equipment to their planes and do pre-take-off checks.

The navigators and bomb aimers then drew up their charts to show the route and turning points with times to be there, expected wind speeds and directions, and heights to fly on each leg. They were thus able to calculate the magnetic course to fly and the airspeeds required in order to reach each turning point and the target according to their time schedules. Ground speed was very different to airspeed so the calculation of wind effect was essential. The run up to the bomb release position had to be in the exact direction, and at the exact height and speed laid down at the briefing to ensure correct alignment with the sky markers. The navigator had to supply the bomb aimer with the wind details as they ran up to bomb, so that he could set these details on his bomb sight, together with the airspeed and the aircraft's height.

Sometimes, the preparation of the charts had to be done hurriedly if the navigation team had to get into their flying gear and be at their planes at the scheduled take-off time. On other occasions, crews were left standing in the dusk, nervously waiting round their machines for an instruction to leave. The pilots, engineers, wireless operators and gunners would have done their pre-flight checks but the navigators had to check their Gee and H2S navigation aids, and prepare for any astro-navigation they might need.

The navigator sat behind the pilot, separated by the massive Gee box and the H2S equipment, in a curtained off cubicle, facing the side of the fuselage. In front of him were a duplicate airspeed indicator, compass and altimeter so that he could verify the course etc being flown and correct the pilot if necessary. Gee and H2S were the navigator's main aids. When flying in dense clouds or at night, there are no landmarks visible. The Gee set picked up signals which were translated into impulses on a screen in front of the navigator, and by tuning onto two different stations he could calculate the aircraft's position. H2S was a radar system consisting of signals sent down to the ground from the aircraft itself. These signals bounced back to the aircraft, and on another screen, the navigator could see and identify rough patterns of built-up areas, rivers, and coastlines. The Germans used to jam these signals so that at times they were indecipherable and useless. Meanwhile, German radar sought the position of our aircraft, and to jam their sets our flight engineers used to push strips of silver metallized card (known as 'window') out of the plane – not through a window! – but through a small chute. If there was time, crews were given a meal of bacon, eggs and chips shortly before the briefings. It would be ten hours or more before they ate again, after a gruelling and exhausting eight hours or so in the air in extremely cold conditions. On return, they would get a similar meal, and before take-off chaps would ask 'If you don't get back, can I have your chips?' hence the expressions – 'You've had your chips'.

With temperatures of minus twenty or minus forty, it was essential to have warm clothing. A little heat was available in the aircraft, but the gunners were exposed to the wind and outside temperature, and so had heated flying suits and gloves. Other crew members had padded half-length inner suits and a canvas outer suit plus silk and woollen gloves. Navigators worked in just the silk ones. Flying boots were fleece lined. Helmets were fitted with oxygen masks which plugged into points in the aircraft, and with intercom microphones and earpieces which also plugged into separate points. Microphones had to be switched off immediately after use, and talking, save for essential business, was banned. Every crewman had to concentrate conscientiously for the safety of the whole unit. Many took Benzedrine 'wakey-wakey' tablets before take-off to remain mentally alert – it was often a long time since they had slept.

However, now and again, an op was scrubbed at the very last minute and the tablets prevented sleep.

When it was time for take-off, the pilot taxied from the plane's parking bay on to the perimeter track and round the airfield to the start of the runway in use, where he awaited a green signal to leave. Radio use was banned. The pilot ran up the engines to full power, holding the plane on the brakes, juddering. On the release of the brakes, she tipped forward and began hurtling down the runway with the pilot struggling to keep the heavily laden bomber straight. The flight engineer stood beside the pilot calling out the airspeed as the engines roared away at 3,000 revs per minute – 85 . . . 90 . . . 95 . . . 100. The tail began to lift and the plane began the climb at about 110 knots. The pilot needed all his strength to pull back the control column for the climb, so the engineer placed his hand over the pilot's on the throttles, and between them, they eased the lever through the gates to get maximum thrust for the ascent. With the enormous weight, only a shallow climb was possible without stalling. To assist the climb, the engineer retracted the undercarriage and the wing flaps. The crew settled down to a normally peaceful trip to the first rendezvous point with the rest of the bombing stream, but keeping a careful lookout for other aircraft doing the same on much the same track.

As the machine trespassed into German occupied airspace it was necessary for everyone to look out continually for fighters. Occasionally, these would be the Messerschmitt 109 but more often a Messerschmitt 110, a Junkers 88 or a Focke-Wulf 190. Later the Messerschmitt 262 jet fighter appeared. All were fast and very manoeuvrable. The twin engined ME 110 and Ju 88 were both fitted with two 20 mm cockpit or fuselage mounted cannons pointing up at an angle to fire into the unprotected belly of a bomber above them. The Germans called them 'Schrage Music' ('slanting music'). The fighters were often directed on to the bombers by radar, but even without it, they could fasten on to the flaming exhausts from the bomber's engines. The bombers took evasive action by going into a 'corkscrew' – diving and twisting at full power, then pulling up (often with both the pilot and engineer hauling on the control column) and repeating the dive until it was thought the fighter had been lost. Similar procedures were applied if the bomber was caught in a cone of searchlights, although rather more turning and twisting was required. Once caught in a radar controlled cone of searchlights which locked on to a bomber, it was not easy to escape. Other crews forgot to watch for their own safety as they gazed in horror as a plane in the searchlights was picked off by anti-aircraft fire or by a fighter.

The way ahead was filled with red flashes on the ground and in the sky as the guns opened up. Fragments of flak would rattle against the aircraft fuselage, or make holes. Tracer fire came up from the ground to give the gun batteries an idea of the height their shells were reaching. It seemed to come up lazily, snaking through the darkness until it got near when it would appear to accelerate and whip past the aircraft (hopefully!) and disappear.

During the whole trip, the navigator took Gee or H2S readings and fixed his position approximately every six minutes and recalculated winds speeds and directions and gave the pilot amended course headings or airspeed. For him, it was eight or ten hours concentrating on plotting, checking positions and doing arithmetic calculations. In the corkscrew, all his instruments, pencils and rubbers shot up to the roof and eventually fell back on to the floor.

On the run-in to the target he gave the bomb aimer the details to set on his bomb sight, and the pilot had to maintain course irrespective of flak, searchlights or fighters, as the bomb aimer called 'Left a bit . . . left a bit more . . . hold it . . . right just a touch', as he lined up the bombsight grid with the sky markers. The bomb bay doors had been opened on the run-in and the draught coming up around the navigator and the wireless operator increased their fears as they felt more vulnerable.

At last came the shout 'Bombs gone' and with the loss of weight, the plane bucked up into the air and the pilot took the escape course which the navigator had given him. With so many aircraft bombing the target at almost the same instant it was inevitable that sometimes they would collide or have bombs dropped on them from one of their own force flying just a little way above them, and to see this happening did not help one's nerves. Adjustments had to be made at the last minute if the Master Bomber in a Mosquito Aircraft at a low level suddenly gave radio amendments to order crews to bomb to the left or right or beyond the skymarkers if bombing was not exactly where needed.

On the way home, vigilance was still essential as fighters lay in wait and it was not unknown for them to wait near the English airfields to pick off bombers as they came in to land.

Crews reported to the Intelligence Section after landing to report on their own experiences and what they had seen, before changing out of their flying kit and going for their meal and bed. The navigator was grilled on his log and had to explain any deficiencies or timing faults.

After a few hours sleep, the crews went out to their planes and discussed with the ground crews any problems they had had. Holes were repaired, engines tested, tyres checked and all controls made properly operational. The aircrews then stood by for the next briefing.

CHAPTER TWENTY-NINE

Raiders:
Four-engined:
Four-footed: For Fuel

This chapter is almost entirely concerned with attacks on fuel supplies. Raids by the four-engined Halifaxes and Lancasters predominate, but subordinately, there were smaller four-footed raiders, and a single-handed fuel raid carried out by myself on my own.

My twenty-second birthday fell on 4 November 1944. To celebrate, we undertook our eighth operation. Instead of candles on a cake, we dropped incendiaries and high explosives on Bochum, near Essen, to destroy the coal mining area. We had to pass very near to Gelsenkirchen which was defended by massive anti-aircraft emplacements, linked to extensive batteries of searchlights. Aircraft venturing off-course at that point had very little chance of surviving. On subsequent operations, we saw other 'kites' caught in the Gelsenkirchen searchlight cones, and rarely did they escape. At this time, German fighters patrolled the surrounding area, to pick off the raiders who dodged the guns.

About seven hundred aircraft took part in the raid on Bochum, and twenty-three Halifaxes and five Lancasters were destroyed – mostly by the fighters. Four of these planes crashed in France and Belgium, which points to the fighter attacks. Of the others, two came from our squadron, one crew being on their twenty-ninth operation with only one more to do to complete their tour. No trace was ever found of the plane or the crew, who have no known graves. Consequently, their names are inscribed on the RAF Memorial at Runnymede.

We saw several fighters darting about on our way home but none came over to interfere with us. On our return to Kirmington the frequent fog was once more hanging over the aerodrome and surrounding district, giving very poor visibility. We were one of sixteen crews which managed to land, but six diverted to Lindholme and three to North Killingholme. The crew which had battled with the two Ju88s on the Cologne raid on 31 October tried to land at Kirmington, but overshot the runway, demolished the boundary hedge and careered into the field beyond the airfield. The mid-upper gunner was killed and three others were injured. The navigator was flung out of the aircraft as it crashed and lay in a fog shrouded ditch for many hours before being found. At the end of his sick leave, he returned to us but without any of his former crew members. He moved into our Nissen hut as the crew who had been sharing it with us were no longer in need of it. He was a lonely and shattered young man. I am glad to say that after the war he became a highly qualified educationalist and we met up with him many times at our Squadron reunions. The death he had cheated in 1944 sadly caught up with him in 2002.

On 6 November, we were briefed to bomb synthetic fuel plants at Gelsenkirchen – that heavily defended place full of ack-ack guns and searchlights. Fortunately for us, it was to be a daylight raid so this time the searchlights would be no bother. But unless there was heavy cloud cover, the ground gunners could have a field day. Seven hundred and thirty-eight went out, and only three Lancasters and two Halifaxes failed to return. Luck was with us as all our squadron machines got back safely. Survival was usually a matter of luck, even for the most capable and experienced crews.

The current strategy was to destroy the German's fuel production and supplies. We had attacked the coal mines at Bochum and the synthetic oil plant at Gelsenkirchen, and on 9 November the target was an oil refinery at Wanne-Eickel, situated between Essen and Dortmund. 'Nobby' Clarke, our Flight Engineer had a bad cold and I was none too good, so our crew was 'stood down' for this trip. However, Max, our wireless operator, and Ray Forbes, our bomb aimer, flew separately with other crews. The weather closed in by the time they returned and they were both diverted to other airfields. Over the target, the cloud was intense up to 22,000 feet and neither the aiming point nor the target indicator flares was visible to the bomb aimers. They bombed blind and, presumably, failed to do the damage needed, as another raid was made just over a week later.

On 11 November, our crew was still grounded, but 'Nobby' was declared fit to fly, and he went with a different crew to another synthetic oil plant, this time at Dortmund. All these targets were very close together and, once again, the heavy cloud meant that a repeat raid had to be made. On the same day, the squadron sent a small force on a 'gardening' (minelaying) expedition off Heligoland, and we had no losses on these three raids.

It was not only the weather in Germany which was poor. It was freezing in our unheated huts, and the mists were so bad that there was no flying from the 11th until the 16th. As I was not flying on the 9th I made my way stealthily to the ablutions fuel store and some coke found its way into a fire bucket and back to my hut. Earlier, I had noticed a broken wooden bench behind the Mess, and I collected that and hacked small pieces off it with a shovel from the fuel store. This was all so that I could light a fire in the hut, but by the time I had wielded the shovel, I had warmed up quite a bit! Nevertheless, I returned to the Mess and pinched a newspaper to get the fire started. I felt no guilt. Two of us were down with colds and, if the squadron could not look after the welfare of its crewmen while some of them were away on a fuel raid over Germany, then I was merely protecting our health by going on a slightly different fuel raid of my own.

While the fire was 'drawing', I went to the ablution hut for a semi-cold shower. It was not often the showers were heated and so we did not use them very much. Thinking back, we were probably a smelly lot as there were no aerosol deodorants in those days. By the time Ron, Peter and 'Nobby' came back, I had a nice fire going and we had a cosy evening – playing Bridge, of course.

We eventually got into our warm beds but we were disturbed by the four-footed raiders. These were mice, running along the shelf above the beds. One fell on Peter's face during the night and Ron found one sharing his bed. In the morning we found that packets of biscuits and chocolate on the shelving had all been nibbled.

The mists gave way to rain and strong gales after a few days and, as a result of complaints by the air gunners to their Gunnery Leader about the dampness of the billets, a number of them, including our Ron and Peter, were officially detailed on to a wood chopping expedition in the woods adjoining the hut site.

On 16 November, twenty-five squadron aircraft took off in daylight to assist the American 1st and 9th armies which were being held up by the Germans around the towns of Duren, Julich and Heinsberg, near Aachen and on the approach to Cologne. We were one of about five hundred bombers which attacked Duren; another five hundred went to Julich, and about two hundred to Heinsberg. All three towns were almost completely destroyed. The flight lasted just over five hours and we lost one aircraft. It was a new machine which I and a pilot had collected exactly one month earlier. The crew members were nearly all Canadians, and six of them were buried in a cemetery in Luxembourg and the rear gunner in the Rheinberger Cemetery. Despite the damage done to the three towns, the American armies found the ground waterlogged and too soft for their tanks to advance or for supplies to be moved forward to support advancing troops.

On landing after the Duren trip, Mrs Stanley was there to welcome us back and to invite us to an evening meal. However, after going to the offices for debriefing, we were told to go straight to bed ready for an early morning op. Ron and I cycled back to let Mrs Stanley know that we would not be able to accept her kind offer. We could not tell her, of course, that we were standing by for another op; that would have been 'careless talk'. We stayed talking for a while, and then our pilot, George, cycled up to tell us that the op had been scrubbed. We had already guessed that the op would be 'off' as the airfield was by then, covered in thick fog. So the three of us stayed for one of Mrs Stanley's wonderful meals much to the envy of the other four who never made it through the fog.

Two days later, we did our eleventh operation which was the repeat raid on Wanne Eickel. It was a force of two hundred and eighty-five aircraft with twenty-five from our squadron. All our planes returned, and only one was lost from the whole force.

On Tuesday 21 November the squadron sent a small force minelaying and at night we went on our twelfth trip to destroy railway marshalling yards at Aschaffenberg on the River Main, a little way beyond Frankfurt. Two aircraft were lost out of a total of two hundred and seventy-four, and all our planes came through.

Although the squadron did not fly between the 11–16 November, the navigators were called up time and time again for briefings. Fruitlessly, we were preparing charts and flight plans and getting meteorological forecasts. Then, with other crew members we all went out to our planes in atrocious wet weather, only to find that we were not going anywhere. They were trying and frustrating times, sometimes after three hours of preparations.

It all happened again between 22–26 November, until we finally went on our last November op on the night of the 27/28. The squadron sent thirty-two aircraft as part of a total of three hundred and fifty to breach railway supply lines and communications at Freiburg which had never been bombed before. There is a Freiburg near Dresden, but this was the one right down in the south of Germany, east of the Rhine, midway between Strasburg and Basle. Defences were light, and 1,900 tons of bombs were dropped in twenty-five minutes. Our own flight was practically uneventful, but one squadron crew perished.

The squadron's last raid in November was the repeat raid on Dortmund, but we were due for some leave so took no part. No squadron planes were casualties, but three 'aborted' – one with a petrol leak and two with engine failure. Engine failures were not frequent – the ground crews all did a pretty good job, knowing that our lives depended on serviceable planes – but an engine seizing up, particularly on take-off, with a full bomb and petrol load, was not a pleasant experience.

CHAPTER THIRTY

Heartbreak

In the two months of October and November 1944, the squadron had lost nine aircraft in twenty-eight sorties. It was about a third of the squadron strength. It was not a good thing for the remaining crews to dwell over the loss of colleagues, or to wonder who would be next.

For that reason, members of a crew tended to stick closely together with their own crew-mates, without mixing too much with the other crews. It was a little different if fellows had trained alongside one another over several months and built up friendships, but it was disheartening if a pal suddenly went missing. We all felt a bit low when it happened to be a particular chum.

At the end of November, 'Nobby' our flight engineer, was especially down in the dumps. Not by the loss of a close pal, but for him, even worse. His long-time girl friend, Audrey, was in the 'wrens' (Women's Royal Naval Service) stationed on the south coast. They had not been able to get leaves to coincide, so they had not seen each other for some time. Unexpectedly, she wrote to 'Nobby' telling him she wanted to break everything off and get engaged to a sailor she had met. It hit 'Nobby' badly. She said she was on leave until 29th and 'Nobby' applied for leave to go to see her, but he was not allowed to get away. It was the period when we were continually preparing for a mission, but only to have it scrubbed because of the terrible weather conditions.

I suggested to 'Nobby' that he should send her a telegram asking her to come to Kirmington to talk things over, and this he did. She came, and we got her fixed up with Mrs Stanley who was always so kind and helpful. How she fitted Audrey in, I can't imagine as, besides her husband and the two boys, one aged six and the other about eighteen months, she had an airman and his wife and baby billeted with her.

Thankfully, all went well between Audrey and 'Nobby', and things were soon back to normal. We were all concerned for them, and especially for 'Nobby's mental state, as he had been a little difficult to live with during the previous week.

It must be remembered that most of us were in our late teens or early twenties and with girl friends or fiancées. Our hopes for our futures with these girls gave us an element of drive for our survival and it was shattering if someone received a 'Dear John Letter'. A crew member's performance could be affected, to the detriment of the overall safety of colleagues. Naturally, if that should occur we all were concerned and tried to do whatever we could to help.

Without warning, we were suddenly given leave on the 28th after our return from our long journey to Freiburg, earlier that morning. Audrey had already arrived so she and 'Nobby' were able to return south together with his broken heart mended.

Our leave lasted until 4 December, so I sent Daphne a telegram and she got leave too. It was good to be home and to relax with Daphne and my parents, as five, stressful weeks had passed since our last leave.

I left Reading for Kings Cross early in the evening of Monday 4 December, and on the train north I found Peter, Ron and Ray. At Barnetby station we collected our bikes and rode back through the aerodrome (thanks to the hole in the hedge), and on to the Sergeants' Mess. I left the others there and cycled on ahead to our hut. As I pedalled along in the dark, just before midnight, a Lancaster zoomed a little way above me, out of control. The engines were roaring at full throttle and at treetop level, it banked away from me and dived into the woods about half a mile away. There was a muffled thump and the ground shook. I knew there was no chance of any survivors. Ron had started to follow me back and he went into the woods and found the plane had gone deep into the earth and all on board had been killed.

It was one of twenty-four planes which had bombed Karlsruhe and we lost one other 'kite' that night – although we did not know it at the time. We found out late the next day. It was 'E–EASY', the aircraft parked in the next dispersal bay to our 'I-ITEM'. All the crew were killed except the pilot who was taken prisoner in Germany. The loss of 'EASY' was to concern us greatly.

There had been one other operation while we were on leave. It was to the Urft Dam at Heimbach (a large reservoir in the Eifel Mountains near Luxembourg), but the target was completely covered with cloud and the raid was called off without any losses.

CHAPTER THIRTY-ONE

Not Easy, Getting the Willies

On the night of 6 December 1944, our crew was detailed to take part in a raid on the synthetic oil plant at Merseburg/Leuna, situated deep into Germany, just to the west of Leipzig. It was our fourteenth op and the longest so far, involving a round trip of over a thousand miles. It was the first attack on an oil plant in eastern Germany.

Our own aircraft, 'I–ITEM' had been damaged when another crew had taken her out on the 4/5 December, and was not serviceable. Instead, we were to fly in 'E-EASY', the aircraft parked in the dispersal bay adjacent to the 'ITEM'. Early in the afternoon we found 'ITEM' ground crew working on her and we urged them to press on so that we could fly her that night. They did so, but the Battle Order had already been prepared, with our crew committed to fly in 'EASY', and the CO would not, or could not, change it. However, as 'ITEM' was declared serviceable, he added her to the Battle Order and sent her up with a newly arrived crew for only their second operation. The long trip would be quite a baptism for them. In fact they didn't take care of OUR plane at all. They had an engine failure and arrived over the target eighteen minutes late. All hell was let lose at them and the fuselage was holed like a colander. Their navigation aids were put out of action and they got lost. They were peppered with more gunfire over Dunkirk (more about Dunkirk later) and then found themselves over the Thames, approaching London where they were blasted by 'friendly' fire! Still, they were the lucky ones as they got back to base, some did not.

We were annoyed that the CO did not allow us to use 'ITEM' and make the new crew fly in 'EASY', but so be it. We had flown in 'EASY' once before, but as soon as I climbed on board to do my checks before take-off, I realized that this was not the same 'kite'. It was not until a few days later that I discovered that the real 'EASY' had been shot down on the night of 4/5 December.

Each squadron had identification letters painted on their aircraft and for 166 Squadron the letters were 'AS'. These were followed by the aircraft's own identification letter, so that on 'EASY' the inscription was 'AS E'. In addition, each aircraft had a registration number – a permanent number which identified it wherever it might be transferred and whenever any servicing was done on it.

I kept a record of all the aircraft we had flown in and on looking up the registration number on 'EASY', I found that she was really 'AS W', known as 'WILLY'.

'WILLY' was the squadron 'spare', an old hack, used for the odd training flight, and, occasionally, by a newly arrived crew who had not been allocated a plane of their own. We had used her on a short training flight and she shook and vibrated alarmingly. A short trip in 'WILLY' was bad enough, but this was to be a very long one. The only consolation was, that despite the trouble she gave, 'WILLY' always came back.

Nevertheless, the thought was enough to give one the 'willies'.

While waiting for the take-off, I climbed down outside and looked across wistfully at 'ITEM'. Then I looked at 'EASY'. There, on the fuselage, in large white paint were the identification letters – 'AS E'. Unconsciously, I began humming the opening bars from the second piece of the Peer Gynt Suite No 1 by Grieg. Its title being 'The death of ASE'. I stopped as soon as I realized the significance of the connection. You might call it superstition, but it was particularly frightening bearing in mind that 'AS E' was really 'WILLY'.

Added to that, we were carrying a 'spare' mid-upper gunner that night – a Flight Sergeant Scott of the RCAF (Royal Canadian Air Force) – and all crews had a belief that a 'spare' crew member always brought bad luck. Our own mid-upper, Ron Hales, had gone out to service his guns before take-off and, while in the aircraft, someone had removed the ladder. When he had finished he stepped out of the doorway, backwards as usual, and crashed to the ground. Fortunately, he broke nothing, but he was in pain and reduced to a hobble. So we had to leave him behind. That was the first 'jinx' caused by 'WILLY'.

There was something else too. It was a rotten night – heavily overcast with rain imminent and a threat of thunder in the air. Invariably, thunder caused me to have a migraine headache, and I had one that night.

Somehow, things didn't seem to be going in our favour. It was a good thing that this was our fourteenth op and not our thirteenth. However, on the 'plus' side, we did have our lucky mascot. This was a little, stuffed, toy rabbit given to our wireless operator, Max, – I think by Mrs Stanley. Max christened it 'Buck' and always took it with him on trips.

We took-off a little later than the other thirty aircraft as we had engine trouble during the 'run up' procedure. 'WILLY' always had engine trouble. We got away shortly after 5 pm. It was already dark, and beginning to rain.

'WILLY', as usual, shook and vibrated all the way to the target. It was a miserable and uncomfortable journey with the constant throbbing of the uneven engines, the shaking, and outside, incessant rain and dense cloud.

On the way, a generator failed, which, fortunately, did not affect my navigation aids or the gunner's turrets, but just before we bombed, one engine cut out and had to be 'feathered'. 'Nobby' our flight engineer did this and adjusted the power of the other three engines to maintain an even thrust – if anyone could imagine 'Willy's engines ever giving 'even thrust' – and to maintain our speed. We caught up with the bomber stream and bombed on time at 20.46 hours from 17,000 feet. The cloud was still solid with the target obscured, but there was a glow to show that the earlier arrivals had found their mark. Below us there was heavy flak bursting but the bursts were hidden by the clouds. The explosion of the shells could be heard and the plane lifted with the thumps.

Unusually, we had made our bombing run from the eastern side of the target on a north-westerly course, so we did not have to turn after bombing. In view of the dense cloud, this was cheering to us as there was less chance of colliding with another plane, as sometimes happened. We continued on this course for some time before making a turn of almost ninety degrees to port, taking a south-westerly course to cross the Rhine some way south of Cologne, and then on a westerly heading to cross into Belgium.

At this point, my migraine was getting worse, and we were in thick cloud with lightning flashing all around. Ray Forbes, the bomb aimer, came back as he often did on homeward legs to help with the navigation and to keep his hand in. On this occasion, I gave him my navigation watch and let him take over completely. I gave him the course to take us from near Trier in Belgium, to cross the coast between Ostend and Dunkirk, and settled back, confident that he could get us safely back to Kirmington.

But none of us would get back to Kirmington that night.

CHAPTER THIRTY-TWO

Who's for the High Jump?

As the plane vibrated its way across Belgium on its three good (?) engines, the lightning got worse. Another engine gave up, and we were limping along on two. Fortunately they were on opposite sides or the strain on the pilot in order to keep the aircraft straight would have been almost impossible to bear.

Excited discussions were going on up front between the pilot and the engineer, but I was merely a passenger and in no fit state to comprehend what it was all about. One of the two remaining engines caught fire and I was aroused into consciousness as they spoke of abandoning the aircraft. But before a final decision could be made, 'Nobby' managed to put it out.

We vibrated on through the storm with thick cloud below and lightning above. With still some eighty miles to go before reaching the Belgian coast, the 'dicky' engine stopped again and inevitably we began to lose height. Our pilot, George, put us on warning to prepare to abandon the machine, and Ray Forbes, the 'acting navigator', left my side and went forward to put on his parachute. My migraine was making me feel pretty groggy, and Max, our wireless operator, thoughtfully took my parachute from its storage position and clipped it to my chest.

Occasionally, the dead engine spluttered into life, coughed and cut out again. We struggled on.

Very suddenly we lost all our power. All four engines had packed up and the noise and the vibrating ceased. At once, George gave the command 'ABANDON AIRCRAFT!' and he put the plane into a shallow dive to avoid stalling. None of us, except, perhaps, Ray Forbes, would have known exactly where we were. I knew we were somewhere over Belgium, but pockets of German Forces were still in occupation there, and we could well come down amongst them. We were actually near Courtrai.

Max came to see if I was all right. We had both taken off our helmets which were attached to the oxygen and the intercom. Silently, he gave me a thumbs-up signal and held up 'Buck' our lucky mascot which he then tucked into the top of his flying suit. He turned away and went back down the fuselage to help 'Scottie', our 'spare' mid-upper gunner, to remove the door. 'Scottie' took a running jump into the gap and was immediately blown back inside by the slipstream. Max indicated to him that he should kneel and roll out head-first, and that is what they both did.

I learned later, that Peter in the rear turret had got caught up in his oxygen and electrical leads, so he climbed onto his seat and threw himself out between his two 0.5 Browning machine guns. He was lucky not to catch any of his vital parts on some of the other protuberances! On the way down, he actually collided with Max. It was too dark and cloudy for them to see one another, but they shouted to keep in touch and they landed close together in a muddy field.

They hid their parachutes in a boundary hedge. Peter had lost one flying boot – they were renowned for coming off in a parachute descent – and so one foot was soon wet with walking over the squelchy, ridged surface of the field. It was about 11 pm, and still raining.

Peter and Max cautiously approached some cottages but as the Germans had only recently left the area, they got no response when they knocked on the first door. At another house, they were taken in and were about to be given a hot drink, when a resistance worker arrived and took them to another house where they found 'Nobby' Clarke, surrounded by a number of young girls who were making a fuss of him. He had been struck by the underside of the aircraft when he baled out, and had had a rough landing as his 'chute had been ripped. The three of them were given a hot drink of some sort – possibly ersatz coffee – and then taken to an airfield recently abandoned by the *Luftwaffe*. They were ignored by the military authorities in charge, and they were offered only cold soya sausages.

Later, they were taken to the Burgomaster's house at Courtrai where they found Ray Forbes, and 'Scottie'. They then realized that the pilot and navigator were still missing and wondered if they had escaped from the plane and if they had survived. They told each other of their experiences, 'Scottie' the Canadian gunner had landed in a railway cutting and been taken in by the crossing-keeper's wife who put him to bed with a big feather quilt, and, according to his story – she got in beside him!

Ray Forbes had not been so lucky. He had come down in a cess pit! He was taken in by some villagers, who cleaned him up and took his flying kit for cleaning. They put him in a black suit which came in handy, for the Burgomaster's daughter was about to be married and Ray was invited to be Best Man. The rest of the crew attended the celebrations and they were all fêted and feasted at the Burgomaster's house. It could not last. The next day they were driven to the airfield at Melsbroek, near Brussels and flown home.

CHAPTER THIRTY-THREE

An Agonizing Decision

Back in the air, the Lancaster, without power, was dropping lower and lower with only the pilot and navigator on board. I groped my way forward against the wind which was whistling through from front to back. As I did so, I became aware of a thud and a thump beneath my feet and I realised that either 'Nobby' Clarke or Ray Forbes had been struck by the underside of the plane. They had gone out via the hatch in the floor beside the pilot's feet, and that was the exit which George and I would have to use.

As I moved forward, I decided that I would kneel by the hole in the floor and roll out head-first to avoid having my neck and head caught by the edge of the hatchway. I found myself thinking quite calmly of my plans, without any sense of panic.

I reached the cockpit area and glanced across at George to wish him good luck. My thoughts were of him and of how he would manage to get out of his seat, and leave the controls, and make his way down to the hatchway while the plane was in a dive, and probably yawing from side to side.

By the lights from the instrument panel, I could see his face grim with desperation as he maintained his hold on the control column. He turned his head, and with an anxious expression, nodded down in the direction of the floor opening as if to say 'For God's sake, get out quick!'

The rest of the crew had been gone for about a full minute, and I knew that I would land some way from them and that George would come down quite a distance beyond me. I was still thinking coolly and rationally. The possibility of having to escape by parachute at some time was something I had come to terms with.

I took up my planned position and ensured that my arms were tucked well into my chest, and my hand not far from my parachute ripcord. Having had engine trouble for so long, we had obviously lost height well before the final loss of power and, since then, we had clearly dropped more rapidly. It was completely dark below and I had no idea just how high we might be. I would probably have to get my 'chute open pretty quickly after leaving the plane.

I was in control of the situation, but fate had not been kind to us that night. When things went wrong, crews tended to blame the 'Gremlins'. But no 'Gremlins' were needed where 'WILLY' was concerned. She managed to create problems all on her own!

I took a deep breath and thought to myself – 'This is it!' I began to lean forward over the hole, still kneeling, when I felt a violent tugging on my left shoulder. I froze for a moment. I looked back up at George, who was half out of his seat, pulling at my clothing.

'Oh! God', I thought, 'he's caught up somewhere and can't get out!' I was no longer calm, and panic took over for a second or two. In that short space of time, it was incredible that I managed to experience so many frantic thoughts. All the time, we were getting nearer and nearer the ground. George clearly needed my help, but if I went back to try and free him, I would probably not be able to do so before we crashed, and we should both perish. I was tempted to dive out there and then, and hope that George would be able to free himself and jump in time. But he might not; in which case he would be killed when the plane went in. During those seconds, I was unable to move; only my brain was functioning as thoughts rushed through my mind while I assessed the situation. I thought briefly of how Daphne and my parents would cope on learning of my death.

That I would never see any of them again, saddened me, and the temptation to jump and save myself was difficult to ignore. I thought how lucky I was to have had a happy childhood, and to have come through so many bombing operations while so many others had been killed almost as soon as they had begun.

George was still tugging at my shoulder, I had to think of him too. His wife, Anne, was expecting a baby.

Whenever we flew, our lives depended on one another, each in our own fields. As a crew, there was a bond between us, and George and I were probably as 'close' to one another as any crew member could be. We got on well together and we had faith in each other's abilities.

Now that he was in difficulty, he needed me, and I could not let him down. I could not leave him to die, trapped in a crashing aircraft all alone, I had to try to release him even though in all probability I would not be able to get him out before we hit the ground. In which case, we would die together, and that was the way it would have to be.

All that went through my head in those few seconds. The panic I had felt when George began pulling at my clothing, had gone. Now that I had assessed the situation my fear had gone. In those fleeting seconds,

I had made my decision, and prepared myself for death. I was ready for it, and once again, I was in control.

Nevertheless, defeat without a struggle was not in my nature, I had not given up hope. With good fortune, we could still both get out, but what had to be done, had to be done quickly.

I climbed back up, and with my feet astride the draughty hole. I reached across in the darkness to try to find what was preventing George from leaving his seat. I groped around him, pulling at his parachute straps and seat harness and tried to lift him. He took one hand off the controls and followed my fingers round his body – I thought to show me where he was trapped. I had no helmet or intercom so we could not converse. I carried on fumbling, but he pushed me off. He was shouting, but I could hear nothing. I found the flight engineer's helmet and put it on. Then switching on the microphone I asked him why he couldn't get out.

The reply came as a shock to me. He told me – 'I've got an engine going. Can we get back?' I realized then why I had been unable to hear him. Whereas there had been only the noise of rushing air, that had been replaced by one of 'WILLY's noisy engines.

'If you can keep the engine going and we can maintain height'. I told him, 'I can get you back! But I'm not sure where we are – I'll go back and look at my charts'. George put out his hand and stopped me from leaving. 'No! Stay and help me!' He was struggling to keep the plane from turning. He showed me what he wanted me to do with the throttle levers in the hope of getting another engine to start up.

I was still standing over the hole in the floor and I hoped I would not fall through – although the draught coming upwards was probably strong enough to make that impossible! The wind was blowing straight through the fuselage and out via the missing rear door. I didn't know it at the time, but my log and all my charts had already been blown away.

I stayed beside George and, occasionally, we got one of the other engines to fire. Fortunately they were on opposite sides so George no longer had to fight to fly straight ahead. After a bit, we seemed to have coaxed the second engine into permanent life.

I gave George a rough course and we made a little height. I recall seeing 2,800 feet on the altimeter at one stage.

All seemed to be going well, until we saw gunfire coming up at us from below. We were approaching Dunkirk. At that time, France and Belgium were almost free of the Germans, but they were still holding out at Dunkirk. There, they had extremely accurate radar-predicted anti-aircraft guns, and we were heading straight towards them.

We were aiming for the emergency aerodrome at Manston, near Ramsgate, and Dunkirk was directly in our path. I was navigating purely by guesswork and my knowledge of the geography. I gave George a new course to avoid the guns, which were still some way ahead. The banking turn was too much for the faulty engine and it died. We began to lose height.

George managed to steer round the guns, which gave us no trouble but gradually we were getting lower and lower. We crossed the Belgian coast and we could see the sea not far beneath us.

As we approached the cliffs of Kent, we found that they were higher than we were. We flew parallel with the shore line only a little way above the waves. I could see the water glinting below the hole in the floor, and, with the back door missing as well, I knew that if we were to 'ditch', the sea would rush in, giving us no chance to get out.

I kept on working the throttle levers and George was struggling to try to keep straight and no lower. We were both adjusting the petrol cocks. My migraine had been forgotten during the stressful moments, but it had returned, possibly because of the cold and the draught. I must confess to shivering from a combination of fear as well as coldness. At one time, I had been ready to face death with composure, but that was when it was going to be inevitable, as I thought. Since then, I was striving to keep both of us alive, which was quite a different matter.

Miraculously, the engine I was working on suddenly sprang into life. It coughed and spluttered, and then picked up a steady roar. It enabled George to pull back the 'stick' and begin to climb. He lifted 'WILLY' up over the cliffs and we cleared them by about 700 feet. I knew the Kent coast well, so we had no trouble in finding Manston. Through the darkness, we could make out the shapes of other aircraft all heading for the same place. They seemed to be all around us, but higher than we were. George sent out a 'Mayday' call and we could hear others doing the same. They were all in different states of distress, and I saw a Stirling bomber with a split in the top of the fuselage just in front of the tail plane, and wondered how it could remain airborne.

George was anxious about colliding with other planes, so I told him to concentrate on the flying and I would keep looking out for any planes coming our way.

As we neared the aerodrome, he contacted ground control and explained our predicament and asked for permission to land. We could see the runway, and George was preparing to make his approach. There were so many planes trying to get down that control ordered us to maintain height and circle. At this point, George lost his normal indecisiveness. This time the usual 'What shall we do, Fizz?' did not come. He radioed back immediately, saying he had only one good engine and was coming in straight away, and would land on the grass.

Actually, both our engines were firing, but there was no way of knowing for how much longer the second one would function.

George sent me back to lie against the bulkhead behind the pilot's compartment, and brace myself for the landing. I was expecting a rough one at the very least – if not a real 'prang'.

George set that aircraft down as if landing on cotton-wool. It was a superbly skilful bit of flying.

He taxied on across the grass, and there the second engine felt it had done enough – as indeed it had. So George shut off the other one too.

I went forward and congratulated him and silently, he took my hand. A little van came over the grass, and stopped in front of us. It switched on an illuminated sign which read – 'FOLLOW ME'. As we now had only one engine, we had to stay put, for you can't taxi a Lancaster with power on one side only.

We explained the position to the driver. He told us to get into his van and he drove us to a debriefing suite. We sat in a waiting room with several other crews, and we were given a welcome cup of hot tea. We gave our names, squadron, and other details to a corporal and waited about twenty minutes until we were called into the debriefing officers' room. George gave them his name and introduced me as his navigator. The officers put their heads together and had a whispering session. One got up and went to the window. He came back and there was more whispering. He then went and stood by the door. The officer in charge then asked George – 'What aircraft did you come in? We haven't had a Mosquito in tonight'.

I'm sure they thought we were spies, or German fliers, for they were not used to having only two members of a crew to interrogate. So, George told his story of having lost all power and ordering the crew to bale out. He went on to say that he got one engine restarted and that he and I had flown back on just the one engine with occasional help from one other. Nothing was said about him pulling me back or my fears that he was trapped in his seat. There was no reason for that to be mentioned. The interrogators only wanted to know why the crew left the plane, and the only question put to me was about the whereabouts of the incident, presumably so that someone out in Belgium could try to locate them.

Notes were taken and then we were dismissed and the corporal told us where to go to get a meal and where we could spend the rest of the night.

Together, George and I had struggled to bring the aircraft safely back, largely due to the loyalty of the bond between us, and, together we had won through.

But it would never do for a Flying Officer and a Flight Sergeant to eat together, or sleep in the same quarters. Oh no! At about 2 am on 7 December we had to go our separate ways – until the morning, when we became a crew again.

The ground staff worked on our plane and in the afternoon, George and I flew her back to Kirmington. She was still draughty, and I stood up front with George, directing him visually as I had no maps. But, once again, 'WILLY' had maintained her record of always coming back.

Whether the squadron got details of our debriefing from Manston or whether George was asked for details I never found out, but the full story never appeared in records. And of course, I alone, knew of the torment of that agonizing decision.

Nevertheless, George never forgot how I stood by him and after the war he wrote me two letters of thanks. These appear in an appendix.

(On 10 March 1943, the navigator of a Beaufighter, flying on only one engine, assisted his pilot, and accurately guided him back over the sea to their base at Predannack, Cornwall, where they just managed to clear the Cornish cliffs and make an emergency landing. Their feat was officially recorded and recognised by the award of the DSO to the pilot and the CGM to the navigator)

CHAPTER THIRTY-FOUR

The Willy Vibrator

Not many people know that our squadron was responsible for the original Willy vibrator. Not that it was of much use as a sex aid. Our Willy was the aeroplane registered as 'AS W' and now masquerading as 'AS E' or 'EASY'. Pilots returning in 'WILLY' always reported constant vibrating. Also, Willy was impotent as they had a job in keeping her up.

But there seemed to be a kind of secretiveness about all this. The Intelligence staff and others above them must have been aware of 'WILLY's' inability to perform. Yet it was never mentioned and never apparently rectified. Nevertheless, by sending airmen up in her, they were risking trained personnel's lives.

There were questions which ought to have been put, and answered, such as:-

why was a blind eye turned to 'WILLY's' problems?
why was she quietly redesignated as 'EASY' without the crew – our crew – being told?
Why did the fitters (who surely knew) not tell us before we took off?
And more importantly, why was an inexperienced new crew sent up in her for a training flight only two days after George and I had brought her back on virtually one engine?

On 9 December 1944, this brand new crew was sent up in 'EASY' as she had now become, on a cross country training flight over North Wales. A report after the war stated that about three hundred and fifty planes had crashed over North and Mid-Wales and nearly all of them were young RAF crews in training, not long out of flying schools.

'EASY' would have added one more to that total, but, as I have said before, 'WILLY' (as she really was) always came back. But in this instance, only just, and not without loss of a life.

At 2 pm, 24,000 feet above Carmarthenshire, flying in cloud, the plane met severe turbulence and went out of control. As it was told to me, all the engines failed just as they had done when we were over Belgium on her previous flight. And just as with us, the pilot ordered the crew to bale out. Four of them did so, but then an engine was restarted and the pilot made a forced landing. None of the history about this flight is adequately clear. For records at Hendon apparently state – 'through a mis-understanding, four of the crew baled out'. The forced landing was made on Fairwood Common, a small airfield near Swansea. However, the four who baled out came down on the 1,800 feet high Black Mountain where Carmarthenshire and Breconshire meet.

The locals in the village of Myddfal, below the mountain warn that if you stray from the sheep tracks up there at any time other than a short period in summer – and this was December – there is the very real possi-bility that you may never come down from the bogs and the sink-holes. Up there, the weather changes abruptly.

At the time, I knew nothing about this crew being sent off in 'EASY'. I was back in Kirmington with only my (limping) gunner, Ron Hales, for company. George, being an officer was – thanks to the foolhardy way the RAF treated its aircrews – isolated in his officers' quarters, instead of being with the others of his crew. Ron and I went out to look at our 'ITEM' and noticed that 'EASY' was not in her adjacent dispersal bay. I assumed she was somewhere getting a completely thorough overhaul. How wrong I was.

That evening, in the Mess, I heard about the training crew having baled out over Wales, and that one crew member was missing. It was believed that he was Welsh and lived near where he had come down and had prob-ably gone home. Local station police were going to his home to pick him up and he would be charged with absconding.

In fact, he had landed heavily on the desolate mountain and broken his leg. The others who had baled out were picked up but the injured man was not found. He was the flight engineer of the plane and his name was sergeant Trevor Jones, aged 19. Search parties went up the mountain several times when it was found that sergeant Jones had not gone home. In fact, he did not come from Wales but from Hucclecote near Gloucester. One can imagine the distress caused to his family when SPs came to arrest him and all they knew was that he had baled out and was missing.

The searchers found his neatly folded parachute on the mountain on 10 or 11 December. But sergeant Jones was not found until Christmas morning. He was dead. And he was not on the mountain, or only just. From where his parachute was found, he would have been able to see, that night, the lights from the village below. Blackout restrictions had been lifted by then. When found, the elbows of his flying suit had been worn through by his efforts to crawl down the mountain side and he was covered in mud. He had clearly been crawling, dragging his broken leg, for most of those fourteen days. He had almost reached the village – but had died in the fields at the bottom of the Black Mountain, at the gate of Pentregronw Farm. Having got there, he probably thought he had reached safety. But the farm had been evacuated and taken over for army exercises, and was deserted. How he had lived for so long was a mystery, but it was thought he would have found water in streams or bog holes, and lower down might have found some kale.

Farmers from the village of Myddfal carried his body down on a gate and laid it in the village church, draped with a Union flag. Later, he was buried at Hucclecote. Myddfal village already had a war memorial with four names of men lost in the First World War. They have since erected one bearing the names of three others killed in the 1939/45 war. But sergeant Jones' name is not on it. The villagers had already put up a wooden plaque inside the church, stating:- 'To the memory of Sgt. T. C. Jones who died in this parish. Christmas 1944'.

Had 'WILLY' been a serviceable aircraft things might have been different. But in my view neither my crew, nor the crew to which sergeant Jones belonged, should have been allowed to fly in her.

'WILLY' was returned to the squadron – albeit operating now as 'EASY' – and she continued to be used on operational flying. On 4 April, we took part in our last op (our thirty-fourth), to bomb oil refineries at Lutzkendorf, and this turned out to be 'WILLY's' last flight too. The crew, who were on their tenth operation, were all killed and were buried in the Berlin 1939–45 War Cemetery.

The crew who had survived that tragic training flight over Wales on 9 December, were shot down during a raid on Nuremburg on 2/3 January (just three weeks later). They were all killed, except for the mid-upper gunner, who was taken prisoner. The six others were buried in the Durnbach War Cemetery. It was only their second operation.

'WILLY' (now 'EASY') was the last plane to be lost by the squadron, on 4 April. I cannot find any record of her being replaced.

CHAPTER THIRTY-FIVE

Christmas Dinner and Bombe Surprise

Much to the relief of George Lee, Ron Hales and myself, 'Nobby' Clarke, Max Leversha, and Peter Turley (and 'Scottie') returned to the squadron from their 'holiday' in Belgium on Sunday 10 December 1944. Ray Forbes was still somewhere in Belgium – or so we were led to believe. In reality (as we discovered later), he had decided to stay in London for a few days and have a good time. (No doubt he would have claimed he needed to recuperate from the celebrations and duties when he was officiating as Best Man!).

On the 12th , we were given survivors' leave till the 18th. Ron's leg was not yet right after his fall from the plane on 6 December, but he got leave too. I went home, and developed a cold (probably through standing over the open hatch on the way back from Merseburg). I saw the RAF doctor at Reading and got a medical certificate until the 20th. On that night, the fog was so thick that all the trains were either cancelled or late and I didn't reach Grimsby until midnight. There, I found a hostel and went on to my unit on the morning of Thursday the 21st.

While we had been away, there had been a change of Squadron Commander. On 14 December Wing Commander Don Garner was replaced by Wing Commander R. L. Vivian, who was a pre-war officer and who had arrived on the squadron a few weeks earlier. My use of the term 'pre-war' is deliberate, as it carried with it what should have become an outdated emphasis on 'bullshit', drilling, parades, regulations, the humiliation of juniors, and pomposity. This new bloke fitted all this absolutely and he completely lost the admiration and respect that all of us had for Don Garner.

We understood that he had come to us from commanding a flying training school in Rhodesia and had never served on an operational bombing squadron. What the Air Ministry were thinking of in posting him to Kirmington we could never fathom. Not only had he never been on an operational flight, he had never flown a four-engined aircraft. Some of our pilots tried to teach him, but he never got the hang of it.

Nevertheless, he was adept at all the pre-war beliefs described above, and more mention of him will appear in later chapters.

As soon as we returned from our leave, he sent for George, and told him that he would accompany us on our next trip. Whether it was to help him get acclimatized, or to see if we were still competent after our recent experiences was not made clear. Possibly, the latter, as while we had been away, the squadron had been on a varied assortment of excursions, and he could easily have had his baptism on one or more of them. On the other hand, it is likely that he had been told of the rumours that our crew played Bridge on the navigator's table, and he wanted to check how good we were!

On the 12th, twenty-seven planes had been sent to bomb the Krupps steel works at Essen, and all returned safely. The next night, five 'kites' went minelaying in the Kattegat, and, because of fog had to land away from home. On the 15th, eighteen planes attacked Oppau on the outskirts of Ludwigshafen, and on the 17th the squadron assisted in a raid on Ulm. There were no squadron losses on any of these raids – maybe that's why the new CO volunteered to come with us, thinking that they were always like that! However, the whole of Britain was covered in fog for most of these days and lots of our planes had to divert to land elsewhere.

No further flying was possible until the 21st when more mines were laid in the Kattegat, and simultaneously a second attack was planned for Merseburg but had to be 'scrubbed' when the fog again closed in.

On the 22nd, twenty planes were sent to Koblenz to bomb supply lines, bridges, and railways to help the armies in the 'Battle of the Bulge' as the Ardennes push was called. The fog was still about but the army support operation was regarded as essential and the planes had to go. One plane had trouble early on and returned to base, but the visibility was so poor that landing was impossible and it was diverted to Leeming. Visibility was not much better there, and in trying to land, the plane overshot the runway and crashed. It was a complete write-off, but all the crew survived. The other nineteen 'kites' had to stooge around looking for any airfield which was not fogbound, and so finished up dispersed all over the country. All that, after a gruelling time coping with fighters, flak, searchlights and bad weather. Many a weary flyer spent an uncomfortable night at some strange aerodrome which was ill-equipped for visitors. Happily, we had not been chosen to go on this one, and, of course the new CO didn't choose to go on it either!

However, he planned to come with us on a short trip to Cologne on the 23rd, but the fog was still too thick and the raid was deferred.

The next day was Christmas Eve, and we were briefed to go to Cologne once more. But the CO was not coming with us. There was a tradition that the Senior NCOs waited on the airmen at the Christmas lunch, and the officers then waited on the NCOs. This was followed by a party. The CO did not explain why he was not coming with us on Christmas Eve. He could hardly have been looking forward to waiting on the NCOs for their Christmas Day lunch, so, perhaps he wanted to rehearse being a jovial Father Christmas at the party. (I think he would have needed more than one rehearsal!)

Just as it was getting dark on Christmas Eve, seventeen crews took-off for Cologne. Two more were scheduled to go, but they had not returned from landing elsewhere two nights earlier, even though the fog at Kirmington had lifted by mid-day on the 24th. But it was forecast to return that evening. Consequently, pilots were taking off as quickly as possible, to get airborne before it came. They were doing 'brake take-offs', pushing the throttles through the 'gate' as soon as they started to roll, and lifting off half-way down the runway. As our 'ITEM' was one of the planes which had not come back, we were flying in a brand new one, lettered 'AS B2'. Two planes did not beat the fog, so were unable to take-off.

The raid was a great success, with the marshalling yard severely damaged as also was a nearby airfield. When we bombed, one of our 1,000lb bombs got hung up on its release wires and was resting on the bomb doors which could not be properly closed. It's pretty draughty when bomb doors can't be closed. While still near the target, Ray Forbes, the bomb aimer, climbed down into the bomb bay to try to release it. He hung on tightly as George opened the bomb doors when instructed, but Ray had not unhooked the bomb fully and it would not drop. George closed the doors as far as he could and Ray came back up. We all knew that on landing, the bomb could be jolted free and force open the doors and drop beneath us on to the runway. We were a little bit worried – after all, a bomb like that could make a big hole in the runway and prevent us from taking off next time!

We hurried back to Kirmington hoping that the fog had cleared and we were easily the first to arrive. I went up front to see what the conditions were like and there, about a mile away, was the green copper spire of Kirmington church. George prepared to make his approach and I returned to my seat. I plugged in my intercom and at once, Max, the wireless operator, called me up and said base had radioed for us to divert to Horsham, because of fog! By that time, George could see the aerodrome. There was no fog. I asked Max to get base to verify, and to check the diversion as I knew full well that there was no airfield at Horsham. The reply was curt, but it showed that Max had lost the last part of the original order. It was 'Divert to Horsham St Faith'. So although visibility seemed OK, that is what we had to do. I found the map reference, and discovered that Horsham St Faith was on the edge of Norwich. As we were ahead of the other planes they had merely to alter course slightly and land, while we had to turn round and cover another sixty miles or so before reaching Norwich.

As we touched down, we prayed that the bomb would not drop. Luckily for everyone it stayed put, and we found we were on an American aerodrome stocked with Liberators. The 'Yanks' were interested in our 'Lanc' – until they heard we had a bomb hanging loose. They didn't seem inclined to help us unhook it – they 'scarpered'! However, by then, our chance of building up a good relationship with them had already been dashed by Max telling them that just a few days earlier we had had a large number of Flying Fortresses diverted to our aerodrome, and 'what superb planes they were'! I had to explain to him that one didn't praise Fortresses to airmen who flew Liberators.

We parked the Lancasters in a secluded spot well away from any planes or buildings which might get damaged if our bomb should fall in the night. We then enquired about some food. As all the other crews had landed before us and we had had to deal with the bomb problem, the Mess had closed down. There was no egg and chips for us that night. Instead, we were given three very damp blankets and taken to a derelict hut where we could spend the night. It had holes in the windows, holes in the roof and no lights. We laid our blankets on the stone floor and got in between them, still in our flying kit. George was not with us; he had been taken to some officers' quarters where, no doubt he was fed and given a drink (coke?).

In the morning, we awoke, to find our blankets covered in snow. In the dark, we had not noticed the holes in the roof, and Peter, who was under a large hole and beside a broken window was like a great white lump on the floor.

We went for a wash, and got some breakfast (unshaven) and then went out to our plane. As we had not been woken by a bang in the night, she was still there. The Americans found us some railway sleepers, planks and sacking which we piled up beneath the bomb bay. We had an audience at that stage, but by the time Ray and 'Nobby' had gone on board and down beside the bomb, they had all vanished!

The bomb was unhooked after about forty-five minutes and while George went inside and opened the bomb doors, those inside tried to take some of the weight, and tied it to a hook with a piece of cord. Max, Ron and I – I think Peter was too frostbitten to stay with us – stood below to guide it on to the sacking as they undid the cord and lowered it (let it drop?). We rolled it down the planks onto the ground and then to the side of the parking bay. There was snow on the ground and we were absolutely frozen. George went off to report it, and he came back in a jeep with an American driver. We had to load the bomb onto the back of the jeep for it to be taken away to their bomb store. Now, the back of a jeep is high off the ground and somehow we had to get that bomb up about four feet. It was one thing rolling it down some planks earlier, but quite another matter having to roll it upwards.

Once the driver recognized what we were doing, making a ramp out of the sleepers, he decided not to hang around. It took us several attempts, but at last we got the bomb into the jeep. The driver was still not about, so we left it and made our way to the Mess for our Christmas lunch. We were given sizeable portions of turkey and cranberry sauce, but then disappointment came, as instead of Christmas pudding, we were served pumpkin pie. We didn't think much of it!

The bomb doors on our plane were badly out of shape and we were told we couldn't fly her back. We had to fly back as passengers in another squadron plane. Once again, we found we were flying in 'WILLY'. But this was the new 'WILLY'. The other one was passing herself off as 'EASY'. Nevertheless, Max was going to take no chances. Our parachutes were still in the plane we were leaving behind and we were given no time to fetch them. So Max found the spare one in 'WILLY' and he and I strapped ourselves together in case we had to jump.

All the other crews had left, hoping to be back for the Christmas Party and our pilot had waited for us specially. Whether we got back in time for it, we couldn't care. We were too cold and worn out to bother about a party. After landing, we went straight to bed.

We had to travel down to Norwich later in the week, in the back of a draughty lorry, with a maintenance crew, who patched up our plane, and we then flew her back.

Sadly, two crews did not survive the Cologne raid that Christmas. One crew was fairly new, and the other had been with us for some time, and were on their sixteenth op. All the crew were buried in the Rheinberg War Cemetery in Germany.

CHAPTER THIRTY-SIX

The CO Gets Plastered at Christmas

While we were away attending to Cologne on Christmas Eve (without the CO), preparations were being made for the squadron Christmas Day Party. We missed not only the preparations but also the party itself.

No doubt quite a few of the crews who hurried back to Kirmington from Norwich after their American style Christmas lunch, did so in the hope of getting there before the celebrations were over and were motivated by thoughts of getting sozzled on plenty of booze.

I don't think anyone expected that the CO would be the one to get plastered, but that was what happened.

During the preparations, a piano had to be shifted from the NAAFI to the building where the party was to be held. The station sanitary wagon, a Bantam Carrier, was used to transport it. A goodly number of helpers were there to get it into the building and up on to the stage. In the process, it somehow(?) managed to fall(?) on to the CO's foot and broke his big toe. With so many helpers it is unclear why the CO was needed to take part, and it was somewhat extraordinary that with so many feet around the piano that it should have come down on his toe. Perhaps it was a deliberate act – by the piano, of course.

The whole of his foot was encased in a plaster cast when we next saw him. Now that was another strange thing. At separate times in my twenties and thirties, I not only broke both of my big toes but five other toes as well, and not once were any toes or my feet put in plaster. One big toe was put in a kind of splint at hospital, but it was not very satisfactory. For some of the other toes, I made my own splints, and carried on working, walking and playing football, cricket and tennis. But maybe the CO's toes had been crushed as well as broken.

On the Christmas Eve attack on Cologne, when the CO was expected to be with us, two of our crews were lost. With the CO now incapacitated and hobbling with a stick, he didn't fly with us and have to face searchlights, flak, bullets, or bombs from 'friendly' aircraft for another seven weeks.

CHAPTER THIRTY-SEVEN

Peace and Goodwill to All?

It was Christmas time, but the festive season at Kirmington was short lived. For our crew, it had not even existed. And our new CO was determined to ensure that even within the traditional twelve days of Christmas, goodwill at any rate, would hardly be a feature.

On Boxing Day, we set off by road in thick fog to retrieve the aircraft we had left at Horsham St Faith. We made slow progress and it was bitterly cold in the back of the lorry. George was in front, with the driver, while the six other crew members and two maintenance chaps stood up, holding on to the tarpaulin supports at the back. By nightfall, we had only got as far as Cranwell, near Sleaford, where we spent the night in proper, warm, brick built accommodation, and enjoyed the luxury of hot baths and dry bedding. We continued the next morning, and after the maintenance crew had patched up 'B2', we flew her back on 28 December.

In our absence, the squadron had undertaken two easy daylight raids – one to attack troop positions near St Vith, about thirty miles south of Aachen on Boxing Day, and the next day to bomb railway yards at Rheydt, near Dusseldorf. On our return from Norwich we found activity under way in preparation that night for a trip to Munchengladbach. This, like the others since Christmas, resulted in no squadron losses.

We went on our sixteenth op on the night of Friday 29 December, and once again, we were in our own plane 'ITEM'. The target was the Scholven oil refineries at Buer in the Ruhr, north of Essen. All crews got home safely, but our flight was not without incident. There had been heavy snow for two days and the runways had been swept before take-off and were fairly clear. But there was a mist hanging over the airfield as frequently was the case. Visibility was only about ten yards as we hurtled down the runway, and as we picked up speed, it was like driving through cotton-wool. Two thirds of the way along the icy surface, George suddenly lost control and the aircraft veered onto the frozen grass. With practically no visibility, George feared we might crash, into the boundary fencing, and he cut the throttles. However, 'Nobby', our flight engineer was sure that the plane would never stop in time – and beyond the fence was a chalk quarry. He thrust the throttles fully open and shouted to George 'Pull her up! Pull her up!' George eased the stick back, and we rose clear of the fencing, and were away. But for those of us in the back of the plane, who only felt the lurch as she went off the runway and heard 'Nobby's frantic shouts, it was a truly frightening moment.

Nor were our troubles over. Now whether George continued to fly with the throttles fully open, or whether the winds changed, I never knew, but as we neared the target I realized that we were going to be five minutes early. Bombing had to be precisely on time, so we had to turn in a wide circuit to lose the five minutes. There we were, sitting ducks over German territory, all alone, and it seemed more like five hours. We bombed on time and did colossal damage to the oil refineries, with no loss of aircraft.

The last operation of 1944 was directed at the railway yards at Osterfeldt (Oberhausen) between Duisburg and Essen. It was our seventeenth, and although we returned safely at just after 9 pm, one of our crews was lost over Holland. They were a very experienced crew on their twenty-seventh op. It is probable that they were attacked by a fighter on the outward journey for the route took us near to the Dutch border. After bombing, we were routed southward, through the Ruhr, close to Essen and Gelsenkirchen which were well-known heavily defended areas. Why our masters should have forced crews to fly unnecessarily past these dangerous places, one just can't imagine. Evidentially, someone back on the base did not expect us back, for when I returned to my hut I found that the brass crowns from my 'best blue' uniform had been pinched. I was very cross, as it was not possible to get brass crowns at that stage in the war, only bronze coloured plastic ones. Luckily, shortly afterwards, Daphne managed to get me some in Gloucester.

The 'Met.' men must have got their winds wrong on this trip. Whereas on the previous one we had to lose time, on this one I found that we were likely to be thirteen minutes late! Anything over a couple of minutes late earned navigators a 'dressing down' when they got back. I got George to put on full power and took a short cut at one of the turning points. We bombed only three minutes late and then found that everyone else had been foiled by the winds and only one aircraft bombed before us. 'Nobby' was furious that I had been burning up his precious engines, and, even after landing, he was still mad at me, swearing that I had ruined them. Who would be a navigator!

CHAPTER THIRTY-EIGHT

Strike Hard, Strike Sure

Having been pretty well occupied since Christmas, we had not had much time to take in what was going on at our headquarters. We had noticed a group of airmen digging up the ground near the offices. They then erected a flagpole. We thought no more about it; we had more important matters to deal with.

Having come back late from our trip to Buer on the night of 29 December, we did not get up too early on the morning of Saturday 30 December. On going down to the flight offices we were told that the new CO had issued orders that starting on the following Monday morning, all aircrew would parade on the square, by the flagpole at 08.30 hours. This was absolutely beyond belief and it was the talking point for the rest of the day. It was unheard of that operational aircrew should have morning parades. Those who had not been flying overnight, rose in time for breakfast and then reported to their respective trade offices for instructions and either went to check on their planes, or stood by for summons to briefings etc. It was madness to expect a crew to parade in the early morning, and go on an op late that night and not be back for sleep until approximately 5 am the next morning. Wing Commander Vivian, of course had never served on an operational station or undertaken any operations. He knew how to run a training unit with drills, parades, regulations and strict discipline, but he did not seem to know that there was a war on in Britain, and there were airmen risking their lives while he 'played soldiers'. A revolt was imminent.

On the Monday morning (1 January 1945) only a few airmen turned up for the parade. Most of the others went as usual to their Section Offices and watched. The CO appeared, hobbling with his stick and a large white plaster cast round his foot. He could not believe his eyes. He conferred with the Flight Sergeant Discipline, and they waited. No more men

123

arrived. The CO angrily hobbled away and the flight sergeant dismissed the parade.

The Squadron Commander immediately summoned the three Flight Commanders and the five Section Leaders to his office to tear into them for failing to ensure that the crews obeyed orders. The Bombing Leader tried to explain that making operational crews parade was no way to run a happy and efficient bombing squadron. But the CO was in no mood to listen to reason. He accused the Bombing Leader of being a trouble maker and he would have him posted.

Now, the Bombing Leader was Flight Lieutenant Arthur McCartney who had already completed a tour of operation with distinction and had done several more sorties since. He had a jovial personality, which was good for maintaining the morale of all the crews and he was undoubtedly the most popular chap on the base.

When the Section Leaders reported to the crews the events in the CO's office, the crews instructed their Leaders to go back to the CO and tell him that if 'Mac' was posted they would refuse to fly. Naturally, the ground crews learnt what was going on and they declared that if the CO persisted, they would down tools. The threatened posting of 'Mac' was withdrawn, but so that the CO did not lose face entirely, he made it a requirement that crews reported to their Section Offices earlier in the morning than in the past.

And so the new year started on a very sour note, and feelings of total disdain for the new CO. Had he taken the trouble to try to understand Station practices in Bomber Command before arriving, things might have been different, but as he had been on the squadron for about two weeks before his predecessor left, he must have observed how things were run and sensed the contented, and therefore, efficient atmosphere. On the other hand, those who are pompous and too full of their own importance don't care, or notice these things.

Hopefully, he learnt how bombing crews lived up to the Bomber Command motto – which is 'STRIKE HARD, STRIKE SURE', for a strike is what he stirred up. And, of course, this Squadron motto is 'TENACITY'.

Much of the ill feeling he had introduced among crews by-passed me as on 2 January, I developed a severe chest infection having had a cold ever since our sojourn in snow covered wet bedding and an icy hut at Horsham St Faith on Christmas Eve. I was admitted to Sick Quarters on the 3rd and while there, George went sick too after slipping on the ice and hurting his back.

CHAPTER THIRTY-NINE

Grounded and Hounded

As I was unfit to fly on 2 January, our crew was effectively grounded. Operational flights with a 'spare' navigator, were not allowed. However, as Ron Hales, our mid-upper gunner had missed the Merseburg trip on 6 December, he needed to do one more to catch us up, and he flew with Flying Officer Thompson's crew that night.

The target was Nuremburg – an eight hour flight into the heart of southern Germany. It was a heavily defended city and, on a previous raid, Bomber Command had suffered its greatest losses. On this occasion, three aircraft from our squadron failed to return, plus three other Lancasters out of a total force of over 500. One of our planes was attacked by a fighter and the rear gunner was killed. The pilot brought the plane down behind the Allied lines, and the other crew members were back with us in a few days. One of the lost crews was on only their second operation, and the other on their twentieth.

Flying Officer Thompson's plane was attacked by a Messerschmitt 410, and a bullet struck the bomb aimer in the leg. Ron Hales, in the mid upper-turret, returned the fire and the German plane exploded. The fighter had damaged the Lancaster and some of the bombs would not fall, but the crew managed to jettison them later. In the meantime, a generator broke loose and started a fire which was only put out after every fire extinguisher had been used. The bomb aimer was in pain from his leg wound so Ron was sent forward to attend to him. Ron decided to administer a shot of morphine, but he was still wearing his thick flying gloves, and instead of injecting it into the injured man, he stuck the needle into his own thumb! As Ron was frozen with cold, he did not realize what he had done. On landing, the ambulance came out to take the poor fellow to sick quarters, and Ron assured the 'medics' that the patient had already had morphine. As feeling came back into his own hand (to some extent anyway) he discovered that he had missed the target!

The next operation involving the squadron was a raid on Hanover on 5/6 January. Six hundred and fifty aircraft took part and twenty-three Halifaxes and eight Lancasters were lost. Two of our planes were badly damaged but they struggled back and made emergency landings.

The squadron sent five machines mine laying, without mishap, but the airfield was covered in snow, and all hands were working with shovels to clear the runway and taxi tracks. It was still bad the next day, but a raid was planned on the 7/8th on Munich – the last major raid on this city – and snow clearing was needed before take-off and again ready for the landings. Six hundred and forty-five Lancasters went on this mission; there were fifteen losses but only one from our squadron.

The MO let George out of sick quarters on the 6th, and told him he would let me out the next day, saying – 'After all, the navigator's job is not a very onerous one'. Although this elderly MO wore wings, he must have acquired them in the days of Sopwith Camels, without a clue of what navigators of the day (or rather night) did. He discharged me on the 7th at 11 am, and I cycled with difficulty through thick slushy snow down to the Flight Office. My legs were like jelly and I felt dreadful. However, George had already reported that his crew would be available for that night's sortie. I told him it would not be fair on the other members of the crew for me to fly in the state I was in, so he had to go back to the Flight Commander and cry off. I went to see another MO and actually found a human being. This one was a younger chap, who gave me some linctus and a tonic and said 'Come back in two days. Don't bother to report sick and go on sick parade – just come along and see me about ten-ish. Meanwhile, I'll excuse you from all duties'. It was difficult to believe that this was a Forces MO!

I went back to my hut and as nobody was about, I 'acquired' some coke and lit the stove. I knew it would not burn for long, so I hastily piled my bedding around it, and some clean clothes, and watched it all steam. It was no wonder we all caught colds; everything in the huts used to get damp from the fogs and the mists.

The squadron was 'stood down' for seven days because of the heavy snow, and there was also a bright full moon. I came back on duty and all the aircrew and the ground staff were put on snow clearing. The runway and taxi strips were all about a foot deep. We shovelled it to the sides of the runway until it was flanked by high white walls. We also rolled the snow into a giant snowball and trundled it down the runway, gathering more snow as it went, until it was about ten feet high! For three days we worked in shifts on the snow clearance, but we could not chip the ice off the surface of the runway, so it could not be used.

A slow thaw set in and one or two crews were detailed for cross country or practice bombing. We were sent on a practice bombing trip on 12 January. The brother of Peter Turley, our rear gunner, had some leave from the army, so he came over to stay with the Stanleys at this time. We found him an RAF uniform and smuggled him onto the aerodrome, so that he could look over the Lancaster. We took him with us on the practice bombing trip. Our wireless operator, Max, had a cold coming on, and rather than wait about in the cold before taking off, he disappeared through the hole, and went in to see the Stanleys. We hadn't noticed him go, and we took off without him. When we reached the bombing range, we found the ground covered in snow and the aiming markers were not visible. Before bombing, the crews were required to make contact with the ground control team. Luckily for us, without a wireless operator, this was done by RT (radio telephone). We got through to them and asked them to prepare the range for us to bomb. The reply was – 'Beetle off' (or words to that effect), 'we're not clearing snow for anyone today!' We took Peter's brother back to base and to the Stanleys, where we picked up Max and reported 'duty not carried out' to the Flight Office.

Max and Ray, our bomb aimer, went sick the next day so practice bombing was 'out', even though the elderly MO would not 'ground' them. The poor lads were trudging up to sick quarters and to the flight offices and the Mess in thick, slushy snow which was thawing rapidly and impossible to cycle through. The cold hut and damp bedding were of no help either.

With Max and Ray still poorly, we were detailed for another attack on Merseburg on Sunday the 14th. This was the place we had bombed on 6 December when all the engines failed and George and I just got home after all the others had baled out. It was not a nice prospect. Take-off was at 7 pm, when it was quite dark. With all the slush on the ground, George misjudged his turn off the taxiing strip onto the runway, and we got bogged down on the grass. We had to wait to be towed clear. George made contact with the control tower to let them know we were ready to go, and then the radio went dead. We had to get out of the way of other planes so we taxied back to our dispersal bay. Max and I began changing fuses and working on the radio. It came back to life, and we reported to control that we were ready once more. We taxied out yet again but as we turned towards the runway George noticed that the compass was not turning. We were fated not to go.

Wearily, we climbed out of our plane with all our gear and made our way to the Intelligence Suite to make our report. We were greeted (?) by the CO, who was furious. In front of everybody, he tore George off a strip (reprimanded him), and accused him of being 'yellow'. This, from a man who had never been on ops himself!

The WAAF sergeant in the Intelligence Section was present and she could hardly believe her ears. The brusque and boorish behaviour of the CO disgusted everyone. Very bravely, she told him what she thought of his public accusation. My memory is quite good and as near as I can recall, she said, 'With respect, Sir, I don't think you understand the whole-hearted way the crews work for the squadron. You have only to look at their records. What about when Flying Officer Lee and his navigator staggered back from Germany on one engine and saved their aircraft? And they didn't even get a "thank you". You can't call a man "yellow" for refusing to fly without a compass'.

The CO glared at her for a moment and stamped off without any apology. He was probably fuming at being publicly reprimanded after he had, himself, publicly reprimanded George. Possibly, to show his authority, he sent us on a cross country training flight the next day.

The day after that was Tuesday 16 January and we were briefed for a short trip once more to Cologne. The CO thought that this would be a suitable operation for him to keep his promise and come with us. But during the afternoon, the raid was cancelled. A few planes were sent mine laying, without loss, and twenty-three of us went for another briefing to bomb a synthetic oil plant at Zeitz Trogliz, near Leipzig. It was to be a round trip of nearly 1,000 miles – the longest we had taken so far. Unaccountably(?) the CO wasn't coming with us after all.

The take-off was set for 5 pm. The crews were taken to their separate dispersal bays in the usual trucks, which dropped them off one at a time. Until it was time to go, they checked their aircraft and their equipment, then stood around in the dark chatting and smoking to relieve the tension. The glow of the cigarettes could be seen all around the aerodrome at the dispersal points. As it was to be a long flight, some crew members were relying on Benzedrine 'wakey-wakey' tablets to see them through.

In all, 328 Lancasters took part in the operation, and ten were lost, including one of ours. This crew had done twenty-three operations. Another plane from our squadron was bombed from above by another aircraft. The bomb tore through the starboard wing, and, somehow, the pilot flew it back to make an emergency landing at Manston. No mean feat, when one considered that the target was about 500 miles away. The navigator, Claude Mason, was a close friend of mine. He was several years older than most of us and in peacetime he served in the Metropolitan Police Force. Some of the credit for navigating the way home belonged to him and he was a careful, cautious, and reliable colleague. In 1953, I was in a crowd watching the Queen processing through London after her coronation, when the policeman in front of me, controlling the crowds, turned, and Claude and I were together again. We kept in touch by phone every year until 1999 when Claude, in his nineties, died.

Poor weather and snow continued for the next four or five days, and, although no flying was possible, we attended several briefings and went through the process of drawing up charts and flight plans only for them to be scrapped, sometimes as late as when we were standing by for take-off. Snow clearing teams were constantly in action till, on the 22nd, the CO informed Group that the aerodrome would be serviceable that night.

In no time at all, thirty crews were briefed to form a force of 286 Lancasters to bomb the Deutsche Eisenweker A.G. Blast Furnaces and Coking Plant in the Hamborn Sector of Duisburg in the heart of the well defended Ruhr. We made four attempts to take-off during the afternoon but the weather foiled us until 5 pm. It was a bright moonlit night and we bombed on green target indicators three hours later. It seemed that errors of some sort had been made in the briefing of squadrons, for when bombing, we found we were about 2,000 feet below some other aircraft and we came perilously close to having bombs dropped on us.

There was heavy flak and our rear gunner reported a Lancaster behind us being hit. Being at the same height as us, we reckoned it was probably one of ours. We were right, but the pilot got it back to base even though the hydraulic cables to operate the rear turret had been damaged.

We normally bombed through dense cloud, but on this occasion the ground and the factory buildings were clearly visible, and large explosions could be seen. Because of the good visibility, we threw out vast quantities of 'window'.

On the return trip, 'Nobby' passed me a thermos flask of hot tea. While most squadrons supplied crews with such refreshment, this was the first time we had been given a flask. I stood the cup on my desk, and carefully filled it. When I lifted it to drink it came up empty. With the hot tea going into the cup when the temperature was about minus 40 centigrade, the bakelite cup split and tea poured out all over my chart and off the table into my lap. It froze immediately and my chart stuck to the table-top. I could no longer write on my chart to complete my log as the pencil would not write on the frozen tea. Fortunately the GEE and H2S were working and we were able to get home without charts. When we landed I was left with soggy paper and a wet lap.

The cold weather continued for several more days and no more flying took place until 28 January, when the squadron sent just ten planes to Stuttgart without loss.

With no flying we took the opportunity to tidy up our hut. Max went outside to clear the snow off the windows. There were only two, at our end of the hut, one over his bed and one over mine. He brushed the snow off his windows with a broom but when he did mine, the frozen glass shattered. I did not fancy spending the night under the open window, so I moved to the other end of the hut which was unoccupied as the last crew we had shared with had gone missing some time ago. They had not been with us very long and we hardly knew them. Crews tended to keep themselves to themselves to reduce the impact if they were lost.

We were grounded at this time as George had gone home on compassionate leave. His wife, Anne, who was expecting a baby in May, had been injured when a heating boiler blew up. I put it to the Flight Commander that with George away and the weather so poor, we might as well have some leave too. But the CO would not agree to any leave before the 30th. 'Nobby' was particularly disappointed, as his girl friend, Audrey, who was in the WRNS, had got leave that week.

The sun came out in a day or two, and with no flying till George was back, I went out to 'I–ITEM' and re-christened it. With two Australians in the crew I painted the plane's nose with outlines of the maps of Britain and Australia, with a lion rampant in the British island and the Southern Cross star constellation in the Australian one. Between them, I wrote, in large letters – INVINCIBLE ISLES, thus conforming to the aircraft's regis- tration of the letter 'I'. Alongside, I stencilled on a bomb for each op we had done. At that time, it was nineteen.

For some reason the CO had ITEM moved from its dispersal bay to another one, further from the control tower and no longer near our hole through to the Stanleys.

We were expecting to get some leave from the 30th, but on the 24th the CO authorized our Flight Commander to let us go from 2 February until the 8th. I sent a telegram to Daphne.

On the 26th the Flight Commander sent for me, in George's absence, and told me to tell the crew that the CO had changed his mind and we could have what he called a '48 hour' pass starting that afternoon and the whole of the next day. It was practically useless, and only 'Nobby' took advantage of it, as his Audrey was still on leave and he wanted to get engaged to her. I sent another telegram to Daphne, cancelling things.

On Sunday the 28th, the CO changed his mind again – or was he just being cussed all along? He said he could see his way clear to let us have four days off from 6 pm that day until Wednesday night, the 31st. Ray Forbes wanted to go to Oxford to see an Australian airman at Kidlington, so I took him home with me and we spent the night at my parents' home in Reading. We arrived at 3.30 in the morning and slept until lunch time. Ray went to Oxford that evening. My hopes for a nice hot bath at home were dashed – the water supply was frozen.

I was preparing to rejoin my unit on the 31st, when a telegram came extending our leave until the Friday night, 2 February. I was thus able to get to Gloucester on the Thursday afternoon till Friday morning for important discussions with Daphne.

On the Friday evening, I met Ray and Ron at Kings Cross and we found George in Grimsby. His wife had not been badly hurt and he was rejoining us. When we got back to our hut late that night, we found Peter, our rear gunner, there with a very badly gashed hand which he had just done, trying to open a tin with a knife. I took him off to sick quarters at once. He was unfit for flying for several days, and on the Saturday we had to fly once more with a 'spare' gunner.

CHAPTER FORTY

Per Ardua
Ad-monition

During the period when we were having our plans for leave changed, we were hanging about for no purpose and Ray decided he would stay in bed one morning instead of reporting to his Section Office. When the Station Police came to check, he was put on a charge and had to go before the CO.

Now Ray was no youngster who might be intimidated by someone of the standing of a wing commander – especially a wing commander such as ours. Moreover, Ray Forbes was an Australian.

When he came back we, naturally, were anxious to find out what had happened. In his delightful Australian accent he told us he had gone in to show the CO 'the error of his ways'.

'What did you say?'

'I told him – "You come here after running a flying school for rookies, and try to introduce parades and a lot of 'Bull' on an operational squadron with experienced crews. Your experience has been pissing about in peaceful conditions, while we're out over Germany being shot at. And to think that we're risking our necks for people like you! You've never been on an op and the other day when you intended to come with us, you backed out when you found the op had been changed from a short one to a long one. When you planned to come with us at Christmas, it must have scared the shit out of you – and so you conveniently had a piano dropped on your foot!"'

We could scarcely believe our ears. Only Ray could have got away with such words. The CO merely administered an admonition. Ray had obviously hit home, and it made up in some way for George having been declared 'yellow'.

CHAPTER FORTY-ONE

Love and War

The years from 1939 to 1945 were full of wartime romances. Families had been split up and numerous young men and girls had gone into the Forces and were away from their home environments. During those days of uncertainty, friendships were established and couples found security and happiness by growing closer together – loving and being loved.

The uncertainties were probably greater for aircrew than for most others. For weeks on end, they were confined to their bases, not merely by the isolation of their airfields from towns or transport, but principally because they were on duty twenty-four hours a day. Battle Orders were issued and briefings took place at any time of the day or night.

Friendships were sometimes formed with the few WAAFs on the station, but the majority relied on letters to or from their girlfriends at home, or elsewhere in the Forces. The love letters were the incentive for the flyers to be optimistic about their survival and their dreams of marriage to their sweethearts when peace returned. Love helped to keep them going.

However, it was not difficult for the young girls with less stressful lives and free evenings and weekends to be drawn into romances with local boys who they could be with regularly, in preference to one they rarely saw. Indeed, some may have wanted a 'second string to their bow' as insurance against the possibility that their airman might not come back.

That was, apparently, why 'Nobby's girlfriend, Audrey, caused him to be so distressed earlier on. Fortunately, by getting her up to Kirmington for a couple of days, things were put right, and, with our leave at the end of January, 'Nobby' was off to get engaged. He did so on Valentine's Day.

Daphne and I were already engaged, but throughout January, her letters had become less affectionate, and they were filled with references to going to dances, cinemas, pubs, Service Clubs and so on, with an American Serviceman called Jimmy who was stationed nearby. She wrote about how much more attentive the Americans were to the girls, and how they made a fuss of them, whereas I treated her like a sister. Even though

Jimmy had a wife in the States, he apparently would like to marry her, and Daphne was prepared to leave off her engagement ring.

The British Servicemen's view of the Yanks being 'overpaid, over-sexed, and over here', seemed to be right.

My letters to her were futile, so when two extra days were added to our short leave at the start of February, I took the opportunity of going to Gloucester to see her. It was not a happy meeting. I was told it was not worth my coming and, although she saw me off at the station, it was a dispassionate parting.

I returned to my unit that night, intending to write as soon as I got back, but having found Peter there with a terrible gash to his hand, I had to rush him off to sick quarters for immediate attention.

The next day was filled with duties and a briefing for a flight that night, so I was unable to write until we got back. I begged her to see less of Jimmy saying he was not being fair either to her or to me. She replied that she would see him less often, but she couldn't help people falling in love with her. I think she must have told him my views, for he then applied to be posted away to another unit, to ease the situation. He was moved at the beginning of March, and the relationship between us prospered.

CHAPTER FORTY-TWO

Vee for Victory

Although we had managed to take off in snow to bomb the Duisburg coking plant on 22 January, continued snowfall and a full moon made it evident that there would be no more flying for several days.

My crew had leave due at the end of the month but the CO vacillated often as to when he could let us go. After much changing of his mind, he suddenly let us start at 6pm on Sunday 28 January. Precisely at that time the squadron was preparing to take off for the first time since the 22nd for an attack on Stuttgart. We were apparently not required, and only ten aircraft took part. All returned safely.

It was the last raid of the month and, because of the bad weather, only nine operations had been possible. We had gone on only two, due to sickness and to George's compassionate leave when his wife was injured in the boiler explosion at her home. But on the nine operations five aircraft had been lost.

February was to be busier, and it began with raids on successive nights of 1, 2 and 3 February. We missed the first two as we did not return from leave until early morning on the 3rd.

The first of these raids was directed at Ludwigshaven, which was heavily defended and night fighters were prolific. Two of our aircraft had to make emergency landings away from base on their return, and three others were destroyed. One of these was the new 'W-WILLY' which had not been on the squadron very long, and another was flown by a very experienced crew on their twenty-seventh op. All the airmen in these two crews were killed. The third plane was attacked by a JU88, and raked from nose to tail by cannon and machine-gun fire. The two gunners, the wireless operator and the navigator were killed instantly. The bomb aimer was down in the nose preparing to set up his bomb sight, and the flight engineer was sitting on the step down to the nose pushing 'window' through the chute. The fighter came round to attack again, and the pilot gave the order to bale out, having been wounded.

All three parachuted to safety and were taken prisoner. After some days in solitary confinement, they were taken to Frankfurt for interrogation. On the table was a bulky file labelled '166 Squadron', and an immaculately dressed and charming German officer began the proceedings by asking 'And how is your Commanding Officer's foot?' He went on to ask about the well-being of each of the squadron's Section Leaders by name!

On 2 February, the target was Wiesbaden with all the squadron aircraft returning safely. We took part in the operation on the 3rd, as soon as we had returned from leave, attacking the Prosper benzol plant at Bottrop, an industrial town in the Ruhr. Once again, because of Peter's (our rear gunner) badly gashed hand, we had to take a 'spare' gunner with us, and he had plenty to do as the target area was defended with massive batteries of searchlights and attacking fighters. We came through unscathed – or at least, without any serious damage. We were one of only nine planes from 166 Squadron, all of which came home safely, although eight of the 192 Lancasters on the mission failed to get back.

On 7 February Bomber Command was asked to provide support for the Allied armies which were being prevented from crossing the Rhine in North Germany by German Panzer divisions near Kleve. This was our twenty-first op, and we flew out without seeing anything but other Lancasters and Mosquitos. We arrived at 9pm at a height of 17,000 feet, but in the darkness there was a danger of bombing our own troops, so the Master Bomber called us down to 5,000 feet and set out marker flares for us to aim at. The town was already devastated from the attacks from the ground, but we were required to destroy the German units and break up the ground to prevent them from reaching some Canadian forces. We did all that was expected of us, but the weather was so poor that the ground was left a complete morass, and the Canadian forces got bogged down and could not continue.

The squadron sent twenty-five planes on 8 February to attack a synthetic oil plant at Politz in Stettin Bay. We got away safely, but one of our planes got caught in the slipstream of another on take-off, and struck high tension cables, causing electric flashes throughout the fuselage. All the navigation aids were put out of action, but the pilot regained control and decided to carry on with the operation. On return, all the propellers and engine cowlings were found to be damaged. The pilot and the navigator were each awarded the DFC.

The route for this trip took us over Denmark on both the outward and the return flights, and also over Sweden on the return leg. Sweden was a neutral country and anti-aircraft guns began to open up – but deliberately nowhere near the bombers. Skilful machine gunners also displayed their prowess by firing up tracer bullets in the form of a Victory Vee.

CHAPTER FORTY-THREE

Per Ardua ad Dresden

After our trip to Stettin (and Sweden) on 8 February, we were summoned for briefings on each of the next three days, but, on each occasion, the mission was scrubbed. It was very frustrating, especially for the navigators who spent time preparing flight plans, collecting and checking equipment, and all to no use.

Having wasted so much time and effort over those three days, we could scarcely believe our ears when, on reporting to our Flight Office on the 12th, we were told we would not be flying that day. With his usual dry sarcasm, Ray Forbes, our Australian bomb aimer, pleaded with the Flight Commander – 'Couldn't we at least do things with decent formality, and at any rate go through the motions of a briefing, and drawing up plans, and collecting gear? It would be a shame if we got out of practice!'

In the afternoon Ron Hales and I hitched a lift in the back of an open truck and went into Grimsby. We were numbed by the cold and draught, and Ron shouted at me – 'Try and look cold!' This was a rare adventure for us. I think I only got away from the aerodrome on two occasions during our eight months there. We went to the cinema.

On Shrove Tuesday, 13 February, we were called to briefing once again. We assembled in the briefing hut, with the windows covered by black curtains, and the target map across the whole of the end wall fully covered as usual by a huge sheet.

We stood for the arrival of the CO and the briefing officers, and after we had settled in our seats, the CO stood and regarded us in silence for a few seconds. Then came his opening remarks. 'I hope you all slept well last night, for tonight you are going on a long one.' The disclosure of the target was always a tense moment, and the CO seemed to pause for a long time before announcing – 'Tonight it is to be Dresden!'

With that, the sheet was peeled back from the wall map. Tapes stretched between pins marking the route out and the route back. We were clearly going to be airborne for some nine or ten hours. However, it was not the hazards of the distance which appalled me, but the fact that I was to be part of a tremendous bomber force setting out to demolish completely what was regarded as the architectural jewel of Germany, and all its history.

It was an operation on which I was reluctant to go, and several others felt the same and made our feelings known. We were told it was something which had to be done as the city was of significant military importance. It was explained to us that the Russian forces heading for Berlin from the south were advancing across the River Oder towards Dresden in an outflanking movement. The position of the Russians was added to the map. Dresden, with its road and railway junctions was essential to the Germans for moving troops and equipment to counteract the Russian offensive.

The attack was to be mounted in two separate waves. Initially 245 aircraft would go in with incendiaries and start fires. When the city was well alight, our squadron would form part of a total force of over 500 bombers dropping high explosives and more incendiaries.

We were warned that if we were to come down in the target area, we could expect a hostile reception not only from the Germans, but also from the Russians. Despite the fact that we were on a Russian support exercise, and Russia was, nominally, one of our allies, she was an ally only so far as we were both at war with Germany. Until September 1940, when Germany decided to invade Russia the following year, the latter had been an ally of Germany, and at heart, probably had aims to conquer Britain. Each crew member was given a large handkerchief with a Union flag right across it and the words (in Russian) – I AM BRITISH. But we were told not to rely on it for our safety.

We took off shortly after 9.30pm and bombed the city at 1.30 in the morning of 14 February. We carried one 4,000lb explosive bomb ('cookie'), and about 2,000 4lb incendiaries of two different types. When we were still some eighty miles away, we could see the red glow ahead of us in the sky, and, on reaching the target, we could see that the whole city was well alight, with flames and smoke rising high into the air. We bombed at 18,000 feet, and our load added to the inferno.

There was some heavy flak as we bombed, and one of our colleagues, bombing just after us, had his 'kite' pierced by shrapnel, and a shell-burst underneath blew one of his incendiaries back into the fuselage. The crew managed to extinguish it, but not before the navigator's chart had been destroyed. Nevertheless, he got the plane safely back home.

Bomber Command and Air Marshal Arthur 'Bomber' Harris were harshly criticized about the severity of, and the necessity for, this raid. For one thing, the city was apparently crammed with refugees from the

East, and many prisoners of war were nearby, but the aircrews were not aware of this. Nevertheless, because of the horror, some blame has wrongly been assigned to them, when they were pursuing what their superiors considered to be a requirement to bring the war to an early close. It was designed to finalize the war by the swiftest means available after more that five years of Nazi persecution, aggression and tyranny.

The raid was part of the wider Operation 'Thunderclap', with attacks on cities in East Germany, designed to immobilize German resistance against the Russian advances. The massive number of deaths and the total destruction of the city must have been intended to shatter political and civilian morale throughout Germany, thereby leading to a swift surrender.

An underlying factor might well have been to impress the Russians, so that if they should be still contemplating aggression against the United Kingdom, they would recognize that our military abilities were something to reckon with.

The annihilation of Dresden was, in all probability, a demonstration of political strength, as well as of strategic bombing, and it must be recognized that it was a major factor in bringing the war to an end.

CHAPTER FORTY-FOUR

Gone with the Wind

We landed from our long Dresden trip just after 7am on Ash Wednesday (so apt); it was also 14 February, Valentine's Day (which was rather less appropriate).

After waiting for transport from our dispersal bay, going to debriefing, handing in charts, logs and equipment, changing out of our flying gear and going to the Mess for our fried egg and chips – our first meal since 4pm the previous day – we got to bed at about ten o'clock that morning.

We were roused during the afternoon for a briefing for a short op that evening. We had been waiting for the CO to fly with us ever since he damaged his foot preparing for the Christmas party. This was to be it. But, as was so often the case, this trip was 'scrubbed', and another briefing took place for an even longer flight than the one of the night before. The target was Chemnitz, south-west of Dresden – again to help the Russians as part of the 'Thunderclap' campaign.

Despite the extension to the originally planned target, the CO was still going to join us. Now that was either very brave of him, or very foolish. This was to be our twenty-fourth op and he must have known that if a crew got into the twenties, it was odds-on that they were likely to go for the 'chop' at any moment. However, if he believed in the saying – 'Only the good die young' – he would probably reckon that as we were not in his good books, he was safe. Added to that, 'the good' hardly applied to him.

Due to the sudden change of plans, the second briefing was, indeed, brief and hurried. When the 'Met.' officer gave us the weather forecasts, we did not have the usual wind details on the map. Instead we were given verbal details and the most noteworthy feature was that winds of 100mph or more were expected in the Chemnitz area. Perhaps through tiredness, I understood him to say they would be from the south, whereas he apparently said 'northerly'. The misunderstanding was to have serious results.

It was a filthy night, and we flew in thick cloud. To make matters worse, my GEE and my H2S aids both packed up. Nevertheless, we reached the target on time and accurately, and we heard the Master Bomber giving instructions to the bomb aimers. The ground was not visible, but the marker flares provided the aiming points, and we bombed accordingly. Our rear gunner, Peter Turley, threw out his piece of concrete as usual 'so that some Jerry might get a headache!'

On leaving the target, we had to fly due south for a considerable distance, and, as I was expecting a head wind of 100mph or more, it would take us quite a time to cover the ground, and reach our next turning point.

At the due time, I gave the pilot the new course to fly westward and, on that leg, we had been instructed to descend. As we did so, there was a joyous shout from up front as the plane burst out of the heavy cloud. But then, an anxious note crept into the voice of our pilot, George Lee, as he called me on the intercom.

'Are we all right, "Fizz"? it looks like large white mountains towering above us on both sides.'

'No, George', I replied, confident about my navigation. 'There are no mountains, it must be cumulus – there's a lot of it about tonight.'

We flew on, and I could hear George and the Wing Commander talking quietly together and agreeing that they did look like mountains. After a bit, George called me to come up front and take a look for myself. It was a bit cramped up there, with the pilot, the CO, and the flight engineer, but I found my way to a window and looked out. Sure enough, they were mountains all right! And a good bit higher than we were. The CO asked if I knew where we were. I knew where we shouldn't be, and I had a pretty good idea of where we were. 'It looks like Switzerland to me, Sir, and those very strong winds must have blown us about 100 miles south of where we should be.' Had we not descended into a valley, we could well have crashed into an alpine peak.

George wanted to climb up over them, but 'Nobby' our flight engineer, negated it. He maintained that by flying south for such a long time, we had used up a lot of fuel and if we used more to climb, we would not have enough to get back. So it looked as if we would have to stay in the valley. That would be all right if the valley did not end in a mountain range!

My navigation chart did not extend as far south as Switzerland, so there was no way I could plot courses to get us back. But, in my navigation bag, I had a topographical map of Switzerland, showing all the lakes in colour, and the mountains in different hues according to their heights. I had found the map lying in the navigation office a few days before, and I had 'snaffled' it just in case it should ever come in handy. And now it had. It was truly a case of serendipity.

I told George to carry on flying along the valley, and if it turned he should turn with it, while I went back to get the map. I brought it up to the front and soon pinpointed our position. I warned George of the next bend we were approaching and then went back to work out where the valley was leading us. I found it led to a junction with another valley running north-westwards and calculated how long it should take us to negotiate all the bends and into the other channel. By giving George warnings as each bend came up, we found our way safely to the valley we wanted, and eventually came clear of the mountain peaks. As we made our way through Switzerland, we noticed villagers switching on their lights which helped to pinpoint our position. How decent and friendly, I thought. It was not until months later that I learned that the Americans had bombed Switzerland in error several times and occasionally the Swiss had forced them to land. Or perhaps the Yanks had voluntarily done so. At the end of the war, I was told that 186 American Flying Fortresses or Liberators were being held in internment.

In a short time, we were back on my navigation chart and we set course in a straight line to Dunkirk, Ipswich and back to our base at Kirmington. I worked out an ETA (estimated time of arrival) so that 'Nobby' could work out the fuel situation, and he was doubtful if we would make it. We decided we could check again as we got nearer home and, if necessary, make an emergency landing at one of the many other airfields in Lincolnshire.

Once over England, we checked our fuel gauges, and 'Nobby' reckoned we should just about make it back to base. We managed it, but had to ask for the runway lights to be switched on as the aerodrome had closed down. Hope had been given up for us. We had flown for a few minutes under ten hours and on landing it was found that we had not much more than a thimbleful of fuel left in our tanks. We had flown over nine countries – England, France, Belgium, Luxembourg, Germany, Czechoslovakia, Austria, Switzerland and Italy.

We clambered out of the plane, weary, but thankful to be safely home after such a stressful journey. However, we were not very popular with the other crews. Celebrations were going on in the Mess in the belief that the CO had gone for a 'Burton'. And we had brought him back!

Surprisingly (?) on landing, the CO hurried away without thanking me for getting him home, and for congratulating me for my competent navigation through Alpine valleys, and gauging our ETA so that we had just enough fuel! As he was not used to operational flying, perhaps a ten hour flight filled with uncertainty, meant that nature was calling, with some urgency.

Five Halifaxes and eight Lancasters were lost on this raid out of a total force of 700. Just one of our crews failed to return; and one crew got back a bit late!

CHAPTER FORTY-FIVE

Deplorable Dicing and Dead Ducks

The CO registered his disapproval of being given an unwanted tour of Europe, by sending me on a cross-country training exercise on 19 February. It was only a short trip, down to Whitstable, up to Leicester, and back to base. It was all in daylight, and it made a nice change for us to be able to see where we were going.

On 20 February, we went on our twenty-fifth op – a night-time raid on Dortmund in the north-west of the Ruhr. Dortmund itself was heavily defended with anti-aircraft guns and searchlights, but what angered the aircrews was the insane and dangerous way the routes into, and out of, Dortmund had been planned.

Instead of bypassing as much of the Ruhr as possible, we were required to enter it from the south-west, between Cologne and Dusseldorf, and then proceed north-east to Dortmund, going close to Wuppertal and Bochum, where we had received warm receptions on earlier raids. The flak at Wuppertal was always bountiful and accurate.

On leaving the target, we had to fly westward, courting attention from the defences around Wanne Eickel and Gelsenkirchen which, again, were well known to us and to be feared.

At our briefing, we, navigators, voiced the folly of the routes, but the decision had been taken, and we had to abide by it. The pilots too, once they realized how close the tapes on the target map took them to certain danger, made their protests and were coldly told they would get practice in 'corkscrewing' as they dodged the searchlights.

We were going to be 'sitting ducks'.

As expected, we found trouble awaiting as soon as we approached the Ruhr, and George really had to throw the plane about as over and over again we were lit up by the searchlights. Nearer to Dortmund, the flak was bursting all round us, and our gunners reported seeing several planes shot down. They were all carrying their full bomb loads, and most blew up, giving the crews no chance. I stayed in my darkened cubby-hole, gripping the edge of my navigation table with one hand in fear, and holding down my navigation computer and other movable items with the other. A piece of shrapnel about three inches in diameter pierced the fuselage near my legs, and went out behind me without my knowing until I found the holes, later.

It was always a terrifying two or three minutes as we lined up on our bombing run, with the pilot holding the plane straight and level, while the bomb aimer called out – 'Left . . . left . . . left a bit more . . . steady . . . steady . . . right a bit . . . hold it now . . . bombs gone!' At the same time it was important to watch out for other aircraft manoeuvring into position and, especially for any which might be above, to avoid being taken down by bombs released from these.

It was a great relief to leave the danger area behind and to cross into Belgium and so back to England. We managed it safely, but three of our crews didn't make it. I believe there were fourteen casualties altogether.

One of our missing crews was on their fifteenth op, and one of the others was fairly new, but they had an experienced pilot who was on his second tour. They were attacked by a fighter but they were possibly hit by a shell from the ack-ack guns as well, as there was a terrific explosion which filled the plane with smoke and immobilized an engine. The bomb aimer was badly wounded, with one leg almost severed. Other crew members applied a tourniquet, gave him a shot of morphine and tied his legs together.

Another engine on the same side stopped, so the poor pilot was fighting to keep the plane from going in circles. The compass, radar and radio were out of use, and they were leaking fuel. Somehow, the pilot found his way back to the English coast and the emergency aerodrome at Manston. On trying to lower the undercarriage, he found part of it had been shot away and the rest was twisted. Ground control radioed to fly out to sea and 'ditch', but he was not prepared to do so with the wounded bomb aimer on board. He warned control that he would attempt a landing, and the emergency services were put on readiness. As he hit the runway, the undercarriage collapsed and, as the plane slid along on its belly, sparks ignited the leaking fuel. The fire tender raced alongside and sprayed foam to extinguish the fire and all the crew climbed out to safety. The bomb aimer was carried away by ambulance, and his flying days were over.

The loss of the third crew that night was deeply felt by the whole squadron, and particularly by myself. The plane was flown by our Flight Commander, Squadron Leader Kenneth Collinson – a man held in high regard by all. His navigator, Charles 'Dusty' Miller had been at school with me at Catford, and we had both been together on the squadron for some time.

There were several poignant factors to the loss of this crew. They had, in fact, completed their tour of operations and were waiting for their termination leave. But this was a 'maximum effort' operation, and we never knew whether Collinson volunteered to go on it as he was still on the squadron strength, or whether the CO demanded it of him. As the crew had officially finished their tour, 'Dusty' Miller's wife had come up to celebrate with them and was staying in the village pub. Also, the bomb aimer's wife was expecting to give birth that night and at the briefing the Bombing Leader warned the gunners not to be 'trigger happy' in case they shot down the stork!

The baby was born just about the same time as the bomber was destroyed.

The major contribution to the losses of the aircrews and planes that night, was almost certainly the foolhardy routes we had to take, into and out of the target area. We were all 'sitting ducks', and, sadly, some of those ducks perished – unnecessarily.

CHAPTER FORTY-SIX

From a View to a Kill

Having survived the unneccessarily, life-threatening raid on Dortmund, we carried out our twenty-sixth op the following night, 21 February. The target was Duisburg, only a short way into Germany, on the Rhine, near Essen. It was an army support attack, to destroy roads and railway junctions to help the advancing Allied troops.

Nevertheless, German fighters were up in force, and, from a total strength of 362 Lancasters, seven were lost, and three crashed behind the Allied lines.

In exchange, our rear gunner, Peter Turley, shot one fighter down. It was, after all, his turn to do so. Ron Hales, our mid-upper gunner, had picked off an ME410 on his trip to Nuremburg on 2 January, and Ray Forbes, our bomb aimer, ought to have accounted for an FW190 two months earlier, before sending a burst of fire through the roof of the Stanley's house, near our dispersal bay.

At various times we saw, or were attacked by, other fighters, including JU88s and ME110s, but on this occasion, we met up with a type we had never seen before.

It was an unusually clear night for a change, and we were doing a series of short zig-zag legs to get away from the target on quite a devious route. The route planners had obviously learnt their lesson from the night before.

Ray Forbes, in the nose turret, was the first to spot the fighter, low down on the starboard side, and travelling in the same direction as ourselves. He alerted the crew and thought it might be a Mosquito, 'Nobby' looked out of his window, which was on that side, and declared that it was not a Mosquito. George, our pilot, anxiously shouted, 'Watch it! – What is it?'

I made my way up front and had a look. By that time the other plane had climbed to our height and was turning ahead of us. It gave me a good view, and I identified it as an ME262. This was a very new jet fighter. I had seen a silhouette of it, but it was so new that crews were not really familiar with it.

It turned to pass on our port side and I went to my astrodome to get a better view and warned the gunners. Ron, in the mid-upper turret, confirmed the identification, and he and the fighter opened fire. The German plane moved round to attack from the rear, but Peter in the tail turret was ready for it. He gave it a short burst and the fighter blew up. I shall always remember Peter's shout of delight, and we were all exhilarated at our 'kill'.

Although ten Lancasters were lost that night, none came from our squadron.

CHAPTER FORTY-SEVEN

Keeping Watch

The squadron undertook one more bombing raid in February. This was on the night of the 23/24th. Twenty-three of our crews assisted in a heavy raid on Pforzheim, near Nuremburg. In all, 367 Lancasters took part, 1,825 tons of bombs were dropped, destroying 83 per cent of the built-up area and 17,600 people were thought to have died. It is truly horrifying that so many had to suffer for the ideals of one power-crazy dictator.

Additionally, not only Germans were killed. Ten Lancasters were lost, and two more crashed in France. We lost an experienced crew who had flown alongside us on many an outing. They were on their 21st operation. Five crew members were killed and the other two were taken prisoner. Our wireless operator, Max, and our rear gunner, Peter, flew separately with other crews, and as Max was in 'I-ITEM', those of us left behind warned him of the consequences if he didn't bring her back undamaged.

At the end of the month, Max received his commission and became Pilot Officer Leversha. He had to move out of our cold, damp Nissen hut and move into the officers' brick-built quarters with George, our pilot. Their accommodation was situated some distance away from ours, so we never saw much of them once we were off duty. It was probably a good thing that George now had a fellow crew member for company, but it would have been far better if we had been able to live all together as one 'family' unit. Our depleted Nissen hut was then occupied by only myself, Ray, 'Nobby', Ron and Peter. The crew at the other end had failed to come back some time earlier.

March 1945 began with an op on the first day of the month. It was to Mannheim, in daylight. This was our first daylight raid since 16 November – or at least, it would have been. 'ITEM' had not flown since Max went in it on 23 February. She appeared to be all right then, but about three-quarters of an hour after we took off, she developed engine trouble and we had to abort. This meant flying out to a spot in the North Sea, designated as a jettisoning area, and dropping our bombs before returning to base. It was a disappointment, not only because it didn't count towards our tour, which we were anxious to get over as soon as possible, but also because daylight raids were so much more preferable than night ops. They were usually safer.

Only one of our crews did not come back. They were very new, only on their fourth op. The remaining crews arrived back at about 6 pm and were told to go straight to bed after their egg and chips, as they were to go on an early raid the next morning. They had to be up for briefing at 5.15 am with take-off at 6.50.

With 'ITEM's engines still not right, we missed out on this daylight raid too. The target was Cologne – regarded by us all as an easy one now that the German forces were pushed back to the Rhine. It was the last of the raids on Cologne and, four days later, the American troops moved in and took over what was left of the city.

With the army support exercise completed in the West, the 'powers above' (who of course stayed on the ground!) deemed it necessary to support the Russians once again in the East. On 5 March, we were sent to bomb Chemnitz once more. This was to be a night flight of about 1,800 miles – not like the Cologne raid. The last time we had been to Chemnitz, we had taken the Wing Commander with us and shown him the beauties of the Swiss Alps. This time he did not offer to join us.

Enemy fighters were up in force, and, although there was a lot of flak on the way out, it was only light over the target because of the fighters swarming above us. We, and thirteen other crews, reported seeing Lancasters going down in flames. Fighters were not the only problem. The skies were clear, and the temperature was so cold that several squadrons had icing on the wings before take-off. Some planes crashed in England just after getting airborne. In all, seventeen Halifaxes and fourteen Lancasters were lost, but all our squadron's planes came through. It was our 27th op, and although we had lost several long-serving crews on the way, there was a close fellowship with those still with us. On completion of this raid Flight Lieutenant Appleton had been on thirty-four, Flight Lieutenant Musselman on thirty-two, Flight Lieutenant Nicklin on thirty-two and Flying Officer Parry on thirty-one. Nevertheless, we all knew that our turn for the 'chop' could come at any time, and the recent loss of Squadron Leader Collinson was fresh in our minds. Unfortunately, the number of ops to make up a tour had suddenly been put up from thirty to thirty-six.

We had more disappointment two days later, when we had engine trouble once more on a night-time raid on Dessau, aimed at the Junkers airworks. This was another trip which didn't count and we aborted and jettisoned our bombs in the North Sea yet again.

Dessau was situated in the far east of Germany and would have been a trip of about 1,850 miles. Two other of our planes had to abort with engine trouble, and one which completed the operation came back with a 2,000lb bomb hanging up in the bomb bay.

On 8 March, the squadron sent twenty-six aircraft to Kassel, but we could not go as George was grounded with a heavy cold. On the 11th, we did a daylight to Essen, as part of a force of over 1,000 bombers, and practically destroyed the place, allowing American troops to move into it without opposition. On this trip, and on the next one, on the 12th, George was declared fit to fly, even though he could only speak in a whisper. Dortmund was the target, and the route was almost the same as the suicidal one we were forced to fly on 20 February, when Squadron Leader Collinson's crew were shot down. Again over 1,000 planes took part, but this time it was a daylight raid, and only two aircraft were lost. All 166 Squadron planes returned. The next night, a few squadron planes bombed a benzol plant at a place called Erin, but we did not have to go, and we started a well needed leave on the 14th.

While we were away, an oil plant near Hanover was bombed on the 15th, and on the 16th, twenty-six squadron planes joined another 267 for a raid on Nuremburg. Twenty-four planes were lost, including three of ours.

One of our planes was raked with cannon fire and tracer bullets which started a fire. Two engines stopped and the pilot lost control. The plane whipped over onto its back, and he was thrown out through the cockpit canopy. Nearly unconscious, he managed to open his parachute and landed safely in a field. He then discovered that his left arm had been torn off, and blood was spurting out. With great presence of mind, he blew on his whistle, which we all carried, and a French POW who was working for a German farmer found him and took him to the farm, where the farmer's wife applied a tourniquet. He was taken to a hospital where he received excellent care, and the staff protected him when, during an air raid a day or two later, a mob tried to take him off for execution. He was liberated when American forces arrived and he was flown back to Britain. In October 1945 he received a letter from the International Red Cross in Geneva, enclosing a letter from the French POW who had found him, and a small packet. The Frenchman explained that he had found the missing arm, and in the packet was the pilot's watch, inscribed with his name. It was a present from his sister at Christmas 1940.

CHAPTER FORTY-EIGHT

Stragglers Don't Come Back

O ur leave ran from 14 March to the 20th, and was most welcome as several of us had begun to show signs of irritability. We knew we were like it, but we were unable to control it. We recognized that it was due to the strain we were under and that after our leave we would return feeling fresher and back in harmony.

I had wired Daphne so that she could get a forty-eight-hour pass for the weekend, and I travelled home, wondering how we would get along, with me in my exhausted state, and Daphne with her apparent romantic attachments elsewhere.

Her letters had worried me for some time, and I was not sure whether she was seriously in love with her American friend, Jimmy, or whether she was using him as a lever to spur me into marriage. I thought she understood that marriage was not a possibility during wartime, nor until my prospects were more certain after demobilization.

In all probability, she did not appreciate what stresses there were on me, with a responsibility for getting my crew safely into heavily defended areas of Germany, and back, day after day or night after night. The isolation of the aerodrome did not help, and there was no cinema or entertainment we could go to. We lived either on the aerodrome or in the air.

It was so different for her. The war had had little effect on Gloucester, apart from the addition of masses of service men and women to the population. There were no air raids, and she was billeted in a private house with home comforts and away from the service environment. By day she was working among lots of young girls of her own age doing clerical work in the RAF Records Office – girls having a lovely time dating the largely American and Canadian service men, and going with them to dances, films, clubs and service clubs. The seriousness of war was hardly a problem for them. For aircrew it was never far from their lives or their thoughts.

I arrived home on Wednesday 14 March, so I had time to 'wind down' before she joined me late on the Friday night. Fortunately, Jimmy had passed out of her life, and the weather had changed from the cold misty days experienced in Lincolnshire, to crisp, but sunny, days of the south. We played tennis, and had a long walk on Peppard Common, just outside Reading. The spring flowers were out, and the trees were beginning to show their new green leaves. Everything was peaceful, and romance was once more in the air. Inevitably, Daphne brought up the subject of marriage now that my tour of ops was nearing its end, and I had to remind her that the war in Europe was not yet over, and there was still the war in the Far East to consider. She returned to Gloucester on the Sunday evening, and we made plans to take a seaside holiday on my next leave.

On Tuesday 20 March I travelled back to Kirmington, having met Ray Forbes and Ron Hales – this time with his fiancée Jean – at Kings Cross. They were planning to marry on 18 April. The three of us cycled from Barnetby station to the aerodrome and we were in bed by 10.45. Trains were good that night.

We were not wanted for flying on the 21st so I re-painted the 'INVINCIBLE ISLES' insignia on 'ITEM's nose, while 'Nobby' and Max stencilled on some more bomb silhouettes to indicate the extra raids we had done. When that was done, 'Nobby' took some photos which are included in this book.

Through being on leave, we missed bombing raids on 15 and 16 March (see previous chapter) and one more on the 17th to Hanau near Frankfurt. On the 21st the squadron sent twenty-four aircraft to Bremen, and on Thursday the 22nd we went on our thirtieth op. This would have been our last if the number for a tour had not been increased. The target was Hildesheim, a little way south of Hanover, where we were to destroy the railway and rubber industries. It was a daylight raid and we took off just after 11am. On our outward journey we passed quite close to Hanover, which was a place Ron Hales, our mid-upper gunner always wanted to see. As we got near, I called to him on the intercom and told him to look out on the port side. As he did so, a bullet crashed through his perspex turret, shattering his gunsight mirror and showering him with glass. Had he not leaned sideways he would have stopped the bullet with his head. He recalls that day as the day I saved his life! On this raid, we lost one crew on their ninth op. One other plane overshot the runway on return, and made a belly landing on the road beyond the airfield fence. The plane was a write-off, but all the crew survived.

We were not called upon to go on the next two sorties. On the 24th we lost one plane on a mission to a synthetic oil plant at Harpenweg, near Dortmund, and the next day, our new Flight Commander was killed bombing Hanover. A bomb from a 'friendly' aircraft above him struck the centre of the fuselage, tearing off the tailplane and the rear turret. The pilot, rear gunner and the wireless operator were all killed but somehow the navigator, bomb aimer and the engineer and the mid-upper gunner all survived. This was an early morning daylight raid with excellent visibility and in such conditions, an accident of that nature should never have happened. It seems probable that the higher plane crossed the lower one at an angle from the rear, while the gunners in the lower aircraft were scanning in the opposite direction. The bomb aimer in the higher plane must have panicked and let the bombs go in the anxiety of wanting to get away from the target defences as soon as possible.

On 27 March we went on our thirty-first op on a daylight raid to assist the American troops to advance into the Ruhr. The target was Paderborn, and none of our planes was lost.

Our thirty-second op was to the Blohm and Voss U-boat yard at Hamburg on 31 March. Four hundred and fifty aircraft took part and eight Lancasters and three Halifaxes did not get back. All of ours came home, but on take-off one had engine failure and only just cleared the boundary fence. It jettisoned its bombs in the North Sea and returned to base.

Something similar happened to us on our next trip, but we completed our mission.

There was no flying on Easter Sunday or Easter Monday, 1 and 2 April, but on 3 April, twenty-six squadron aircraft made up a force of 247 Lancasters for a daylight raid on a large military barracks at Nordhausen mid-way between Kassel and Leipzig. The first of our planes took off at 12.47 hours and the target time was to be 16.15.

At 12.15 we started checking our engines and equipment. One engine was giving trouble over and over again. The ground crew worked on it frantically. They were still at it when all the other aircraft had left. At last it was declared serviceable, and we rumbled down the runway at 13.15. It meant we would have to work the engines hard to catch up with the rest of the stream. To be lagging behind once we were over Germany – in daylight – would be asking for trouble from fighters and gun emplacements.

Just as we were about to rise off the runway, the wayward engine seized up and, with our bombs and fuel tanks full, George did well to get the plane off the ground. There were tall trees at the end of the runway, and it was questionable whether we would make enough height to clear them. Somehow, George managed to lift her over their top branches. He circled and landed. The ground crew found foliage on the tailplane. It had been a near thing, and some of those watching on the ground thought we had not made it. The ambulance and crash tender were both out looking for us.

The ground engineers began working on the engines again, and we were picked up by transport and taken back to the control tower. After making his report, George was told to keep the crew standing by in case the plane could be made serviceable.

Around half an hour later, the engineers reported that the plane was now fit to fly. We were ordered to continue with the operation and, despite our objections that we were too far behind the bombing force, we were made to go.

Before that, the plane had to be topped up with fuel and the engines and equipment tested all over again. The remainder of the planes had been gone for an hour and a half. If we were to follow the authorized flight plan, we would be on our own over Germany, and bombing about an hour after the others.

We had done sufficient operations to know what happened to stragglers. They were easy targets and they were unlikely to get back.

While the engines and equipment were being tested, I sat at my navigation table working out whether we could take an unofficial short cut to join up with the stream somewhere near the target. I discussed this with George and 'Nobby', our flight engineer, and, although we would be well off the official track and liable to attack from our own defences as well as enemy fighters, we agreed it was our best option.

Fortunately there was thick cloud which protected us visually from the fighters, but there was always the possibility that they might latch on to us by radar. We joined up with the main stream only a few miles from Nordhausen, and bombed right on time, using our H2S radar as the cloud was too dense to see target markers. We had had no trouble and we returned safely.

At debriefing I was reprimanded severely for not sticking to the set route. I pointed out that my instructions were to bomb at 16.15 and that is what we did – as a result of skilful navigation on my part. I also made clear what I thought of the CO for forcing us to take off so long after the rest of the squadron and in an aircraft which it was now known had a 'dodgy' engine. It was as good as sending us to our certain deaths, for we all knew that stragglers did not come back.

Perhaps the CO with so little experience of a bombing squadron was unaware of this, and no one was bold enough to put him wise. He was not a man who would relish having his decisions queried.

It may be that this operation had been designated as a 'maximum effort' one by Group and if the CO had committed himself to send a definite number of aircraft, he might not have wanted to lose face by not doing so. Putting it another way, he might have been more interested in the number which went out, rather than the number which got back; or in his status than our lives.

It is difficult to have decent thoughts of this man and we could not help but think that as we were so near the completion of our tour, we would shortly be lost to the squadron, and as such we might have been thought expendable.

At all events, we could not have been the CO's favourite crew. When he flew with us, we were criticised for calling up the pilot by his first name instead of saying 'navigator to pilot' as in the text books. He was also unhappy about dropping into an Alpine valley, despite the wonderful scenery. Moreover, he had accused our George of being 'yellow', and he would not have enjoyed our bomb aimer insinuating that he had a piano dropped on his foot to avoid coming on a very long operational flight.

It is not in my nature to think badly of people, but the manner and behaviour of this man can only be called despicable.

I had ensured that an expensive aeroplane had not been destroyed, and a whole crew had been saved from what could easily have been 'curtains'; for stragglers don't come back.

CHAPTER FORTY-NINE

No More – No Thanks!

Our thirty-fourth operation was an attack on fuel refineries at Lutzkendorf the following night, Wednesday 4 April.

Visibility, this time, was good and, because of excellent target marking, the bombing was pretty accurate. One of our crews on their tenth op was lost over Germany. They were flying in 'E-EASY', which was formerly the untrustworthy 'W-WILLY' (from which our crew had to bale out on 6 December) but which was now properly operational.

One other crew had to make a forced landing in France, and one crew on their very first op returned safely but as they were preparing to land the pilot saw another aircraft attempting to come in above him. He put his machine into a dive at full power but he was too low and crashed into high ground on the outskirts of Barnetby, about three miles away. The pilot and the rear gunner survived, but the other five crew members were killed.

We were anxious to complete our remaining two missions to complete our tour, but it looked as if we might have to wait some time, as George Lee, our pilot, went into sick quarters with yet another cold and chest infection on 7 April.

However, on Monday 9 April, we learnt that the number of ops for a tour was now to be only thirty-three instead of thirty-six. As we had completed thirty-four our tour was over. The reduction was made in a general announcement to all crews in the Flight Office. Without any definite confirmation that we had finished, we just had to assume so.

Normally, when a crew came back from their last operation, they landed in high spirits and with an exultant feeling of elation. In our case, we had come back, unknowingly, from our final trip. We missed out on the usual joy of jumping down on to terra firma for the very last time. Instead, my own personal feeling was that we had suddenly been made redundant.

Perhaps we would have felt better if our CO had congratulated us by saying something like – 'Well done, chaps! Now that the number of ops has been reduced, your tour has automatically been completed. I give you my thanks for your efforts on behalf of the Squadron, which have undoubtedly contributed to the war being nearly over'. Instead, we were left to work out for ourselves that we had finished.

My underlying feeling was one of sadness, yet thankful that my life had been spared. I made my way alone to the village church in a subdued mood. The church was locked, so I said my prayers in the churchyard, thanking God for my survival without wounds or injuries, before walking slowly back the two miles to my cold Nissen hut.

I wanted to let my parents and Daphne know that my ops were over, but the Station was on stand-by, with crews being briefed for that night's mission. Consequently, no outgoing calls were permissible from the area, and no telegrams could be sent. I had to post letters to them instead.

In the evening, I went with Peter Turley, our rear gunner, into Grimsby so that he could let some friends know the good news. We celebrated by going to the theatre. It was only the second time I had had the opportunity to leave the station and go into Grimsby. On our return to the aerodrome, we found 'Nobby', Ray and Ron the worse for drink in the Mess. They rather overdid it and eventually came to bed reeling and rowdy. At midnight, two, at least, were outside being sick. They had, of course, been celebrating a momentous occasion in what was quite a usual manner. However, the suffering afterwards hardly seemed worth it.

The war in Europe was not quite over, and the squadron took part in six more operations before the end. There were no more losses as German defences had become almost non existent.

On 9 April the target was Kiel, and on the 10th, a railway complex at Plauen about forty miles south of Leipzig. On Saturday 14 April Potsdam was bombed and on the 18th the naval base on the island of Heligoland was hammered. A proposed attack on Bremen on the 22nd was called off before any planes bombed because of the smoke and dust which obscured the target. British troops were down there about to go in. The last raid of the war by our squadron was on Wednesday 25 April to destroy an SS military barracks at Hitler's headquarters at Berchtesgaden.

George came out of sick bay quite soon, and he, Max, 'Nobby', Ron and Peter went on leave a few days later. Ray Forbes and I remained on the Station awaiting an interview with the Wing Commander for assessment for commissions. Not surprisingly, neither of us was successful! Meanwhile, Ron Hales married his Jean on 18 April, but Ray and I were unable to be there. We finally left Kirmington on 25 April.

I took all my kit home, collected my tennis racquet and swimming costume, and travelled to Babbacombe in Devon to start my planned seaside holiday with Daphne, from 28 April to 6 May. However, there was no tennis and no swimming. It snowed!

We enjoyed the peace of Babbacombe, and real peace came two days after our return, with VE DAY. By then, Daphne was back in Gloucester, and I was at home listening to the celebrations on the radio. Strangely, I felt run-down and listless.

CHAPTER FIFTY

Assessing the Cost

I suffered a breakdown in my health, shortly after ending my tour of ops. It took the form of a severe depression. While flying in Bomber Command I was perfectly fit and competent. There was never any indication that I might be losing my grip.

Once the war in Europe was over, I became completely negative. I was unable to concentrate for long and I lost interest in nearly all activities. My appetite was gone, and I was nearly always tired, and yet I slept badly. My weight fell by nearly two stones, and I was easily upset. Often, I was close to tears and day after day, I had agonizing headaches, frequently followed by retching and vomiting.

The unhappiness caused by depression is difficult to imagine for those who have not experienced it.

The stress of going on bombing raids was scarcely noticeable at the time, and, indeed, we were more depressed by the living conditions on the aerodrome. At Kirmington, during our stay, mist, fogs, snow, ice, and prolonged rain were commonplace. There was very little fuel available to warm our cold Nissen huts or the crew huts where we congregated by day. Our bedding and clothing steamed on the occasions when we found some fuel to light our stove in the centre of our hut, and regularly we were going down with colds.

Bombing crews could hardly be expected to be at their best living in such uncomfortable, health-threatening conditions, and there were no entertainment facilities laid on to maintain morale.

When not flying at night, most crews congregated in the Mess where it was warmer, and where they drank excessively, probably to drown their unhappiness and their fears. Drink held no fascination for me, and I felt I had a responsibility as my crew's navigator to have a clear head in order to concentrate wholeheartedly in the air for hours at a stretch.

However, in the circumstances, recourse to drink could hardly be condemned. The aircrews went through months of continual debilitating experiences, and every time they took off they knew that there was a strong chance that they might not come back, or that they might be so badly hurt that life would never be the same again.

Their mental approach to each operation had to be adjusted. Bombing civilians could, at times, be distasteful, and, by and large, aircrews did not enjoy what they had to do. It was largely a matter of steeling oneself to go to blow others to bits, and to face the fear of being blown to smithereens oneself. Generally, one always thought that if anyone was going to get the 'chop', it would be some poor sod in another crew. To help us to overcome our fears we had the comradeship of our fellow crew members, with great trust in them, and particularly, also, in the hard-working ground mechanics who kept our aircraft in an airworthy condition.

At least with bombing from a height, we were spared the sight of women and children being burned or killed, or hearing their screams. One had to accept that masses of civilians were engaged on war work in aircraft and munitions factories, and in providing supply services, and, as such, their destruction and persecution was as necessary as the attacks on military personnel or installations. Moreover, lines of communication or transportation could not be destroyed without involving civilians.

The aim of war was the defeat of the enemy, and air bombardment was a means recognized by both sides. Thus, air raids were of high value for breaking down civilian morale and the disruption of civilian life. It was but one small step further to instigate the fire storm of Dresden which was criticized so much. Such critics should bear in mind, gratefully, that the ruthless war-like leaders of Germany and Japan were forced to bring THEIR wars to early termination as a result of the air power and the bombing of Dresden, Hiroshima and Nagasaki, horrible though they were.

It should not be forgotten that the airmen involved paid a price too. In fighting the war in Europe, RAF Bomber Command lost 55,000 aircrew members, of whom 47,000 were killed on operational raids and 8,000 in training accidents. Bombing operations were mostly carried out in dark-ness, in the early morning, when the human body is not normally regarded as being at its best. Yet these airmen had the courage and forti-tude to overcome their fears and the hardships both by day and by night.

The insignia of 166 Squadron was a fierce-looking bulldog above the word 'TENACITY'. Our crews who pressed on with missions when under severe attack, or with damage to their aircraft, certainly lived up to the emblem of their squadron.

Out of 199 Lancaster aircraft which served the squadron, 149 either crashed or were registered as missing. Nearly 1,000 lives were lost, and some survivors were left physically disabled.

Each year until 2003 a large number of survivors attended a church service, followed by a remembrance service at the squadron memorial in the village of Kirmington, to honour and thank those courageous lads who, unfortunately, did not live to see the results of their efforts. The services were discontinued only when the number of survivors declined or they were forced to forego attendance by reason of age or disabilities.

To my knowledge there are few other squadrons who continued such services or reunions for so long. It speaks volumes for the fellowship that binds the air and ground crews of those war years and the respect in which they hold their less fortunate colleagues, who never made it back to base.

A great deal of time and hard work went into the organization and arrangements for those annual reunions, and these were cheerfully and efficiently carried out by Jim Wright, a wireless operator who served on the squadron while I was there. His whole family and a few ex-squadron colleagues also lent a hand and their efforts were wholeheartedly appreciated by us all.

CHAPTER FIFTY-ONE

Down and Out

Following the end of the war in Europe, I was posted to an Aircrew Allocation Centre at Catterick on 17 May 1945 and I was accepted for training as a navigator/observer in Transport Command. With the Japanese war continuing, I was scheduled for service in the Far East. I waited until the end of June when I joined the Transport Command Operational Unit at Bramcote, near Nuneaton, where the course was a gruelling one. Besides the usual subjects, a great deal of attention was given to mathematical tests and trigonometrical problems.

My nervous debility was still worrying me and I found concentration on the intensive studies difficult. I, and three others, failed to qualify and we were sent to a reallocation centre at Lissett, near Bridlington. Here I was reclassified as a Clerk/GD (General Duties) and I had to wait until 10 October for a posting. On that date I reported to a Personnel Disposal Centre at Blackpool, and learnt that I was being posted to the Far East, even though the Japanese war had ended two months earlier.

At this point, Daphne and I decided that we should marry before I went abroad, and the big day was in Reading on Thursday 18 October, by Special Licence. We had no honeymoon. I had to be back in Blackpool on the Sunday.

My depressive illness was no better, and one day I collapsed in the kitting-out centre and was directed to see the Medical Officer in the morning. That night I ran into Ron Hales, my former mid-upper gunner, who I did not know was in Blackpool. Ron insisted on coming with me to see the MO and he went in before me and must have told the doctor a good story. The outcome was that I was taken off the overseas posting and on 1 January 1946 I reported to Technical Training Headquarters at Brampton, near Huntingdon.

In dealing with my posting, Records Office queried my rank of Flight Sergeant. They notified my unit that I had been promoted to Warrant Officer on 26 January 1945 when still on ops, but the squadron never posted it in Orders! I had to stay a Flight Sergeant until it went up in Orders at Brampton on 8 February – over a year late.

I was still being paid as a flight sergeant so there was a lot of back pay due to me, but, for the first two months I was at Brampton, there was no pay for me when I attended the pay parades for the clerical staff. I was told it was because my pay details were slow coming through. Eventually I saw a WAAF in the pay section who accused me of not attending pay parades, as my pay had always been there awaiting me. She showed me the records, and sure enough, my name was on the sheets every time. I then noticed that the lists were not for the clerical grades, but for nursing officers. My classification as 'NO/Clerk/ GD' stood for 'Navigator Observer/Clerk GD'. Confusing for the poor girl.

Having now officially become a Warrant Officer, I had to take my turns as Duty Officer, and on one weekend duty I had to march a large squad of German POWs from their caged enclosure on the camp to the church service about two miles away in the centre of the village. It was somewhat farcical that these prisoners were kept on the camp under lock and key and in a wired enclosure, and then they were let out to be marched under the supervision of just one warrant officer to the local church and back.

When the service was over their Camp Commandant formed them up to march them back and informed me that two of his men were missing. He understood that they were still in the church and he suggested that I should go in to get them out. I pointed out that while I was away all the others might abscond and I sent him back to find his men. After some minutes, he returned with the two absentees. He walked up to me, and nudged my arm, saying with a wink – 'And vot vould you haf done if I had not returned also?' He recognized the ridiculousness of the arrangement.

For the first few months on the unit, I remained on medication as a sedative. This was phenobarbitone which made my reactions slow and I was quite lethargic. I was replacing a warrant officer observer who was being demobbed, and one of the first things he asked me was whether I played football. He ran the station team and played in goal. So, in my first week I was helped to settle in and although nowhere near my best I played in most games thereafter. I realized that my poor displays were due to the phenobarbitone, so I stopped taking the tablets and I was back to normal. About five years later my son was born in the Royal Berks Hospital in Reading and when I went to see him for the first time, there was one other new father doing the same thing. After a while he said he thought he recognized me and asked if I had been in the RAF at Brampton. On learning that I had, he said – 'I thought that's where I must have seen you. You were the outside left in a team that played the German POWs – I was the referee!'

It was easy for me to settle in at Brampton for it was a very happy station staffed by a good number of ex-aircrew. Officers and other ranks were friendly and helpful. Officers returning in cars from leaves used to stop and pick up airmen walking from the station. They suddenly stopped doing so, and orders were issued that saluting of officers within the camp was to be the norm.

At the same time, at the end of June 1946, it was announced that all NCO aircrew were to be downgraded to the rank of sergeant until the end of June 1947 when they would have to revert to AC2 or whatever was their basic grade in their reallocated trade at that time. This downgrading applied to NCOs only. Officers were to retain their commissioned ranks even though they were no longer flying and even if they had never got as far as operational flying. The officers could also be promoted. Such was the way the RAF thanked the airmen who had contributed so much to the finalization of the war. These NCOs were the people who had volunteered for aircrew duties for the duration of the war. They were now having to wait for demobilization, and, unless they were commissioned, they were to be stripped of their rank. This was apparently an Air Ministry decision, so perhaps the RAF was not to blame. Perhaps the fault was with the newly-elected Labour government.

My particular job in Technical Training HQ was to assist a Flying Officer (ex wireless op/air gunner) – who shortly was promoted to Flight Lieutenant – on Manning Control, relating to strengths and postings to all Technical Training units. It involved telephoning, sending signals, and correspondence, and collecting and collating data on movements of personnel. Suddenly, my contacts at other units had to address me as Sergeant instead of Warrant Officer, and they probably thought I had been Court Martialled for some really serious crime.

At the same time our working hours were changed and we had to do half an hour more than the officers each day, and go on morning parades before work.

Shortly before the downgrading, I returned from a weekend leave, and on the train I met a fellow warrant officer who told me he was reporting for duty at Brampton. He was wearing his greatcoat, so I could not tell if he was wearing aircrew insignia, but, quite wrongly, I assumed he was one of us. He had the most weird ideas about life generally. When I wrote to Daphne that night I reported that he was 'not quite right in the head'. He turned out to be the new Warrant Officer (Disciplinary) for the station, with the nickname 'The Killer', as a result of an airman collapsing and dying when on punishment drill. He instigated all kinds of petty restrictions and parades, and was utterly disliked. On five separate occasions I discovered fires either in his hut or just outside. These I put out with an extinguisher, and wondered if the pay section WAAF would be flummoxed if I remustered as a firefighter.

The flight lieutenant I worked with did not want leave at Christmas and let me have seven days. I also had a thirty-six-hour weekend pass due to me, so he agreed that I could add the two together. However, when I put in my application to the office, 'The Killer' insisted that I took the thirty-six-hour pass and returned to the camp before immediately going off for the seven days. His mind was not open to logic or reason, and as Ray Forbes, my bomb aimer, used to say when dealing with RAF permanent staff – 'You can't argue with the ignorant'. Having had so much mathematical training, I managed to run the two together with the loss of only a few hours.

On my return, I found 'The Killer' had introduced more 'bull'. He had planned to introduce a special new parade that morning around the station flagpole but, at the last moment, it could not take place because of the atrocious weather. Strangely there was no sign of the man himself. I was told he was in the sick bay. He had been found rolling in agony on his office floor with some sort of stomach trouble. One couldn't help wondering . . .

I came out of the Air Force on 3 February 1947 (with demob leave to follow), and was not sorry to do so. Since leaving my operational squadron, the RAF (or at least that part of it that I was in) had reverted to restrictive, illogical, disciplinary ways which we had observed when we first joined up. Those with any sort of power were much like the Hitler we had just been fighting. They were, in fact, known as 'little Hitlers'.

Nevertheless, there were good times as well as bad during the four and a half years I served in the Air Force. It was the comradeship and unselfish attitudes of our fellow aircrews who went 'dicing' in hazardous conditions, which I recall as the good times – not forgetting the humour of a certain German POW Commandant. Per Ardua ad-ulterated.

APPENDIX 1

Letters written to Don Feesey from George Lee

" .. they would pack up flying for good.

 The "happy event" has not yet arrived, but should take place in about three weeks time. Anne and I are both looking forward to it, so I will let you know as soon as possible.

I think that's all for now, so kind regards to Daphne and your family, and many thanks for your excellent navigation and steadying influebce on the rest of us, when things went " hay wire", and thanks for sticking with me over Belgium on Dec 6th 1944 - that is something I shall never fotget you for.

 All best wishes for the future and keep in touch.

  Yours ever,

   George (Item Lee)

PHONE
HILLSIDE 51.

ROSEMOUNT,

HILLSIDE,

MONTROSE.

ANGUS.

they would pack up flying for
good.

The "happy event" has not yet
arrived, but should take place
in about three weeks time, and
and we are both looking forward
to it, so I will let you know
as soon as possible.

I think that is all for now,
so kind regards to Squire and
your family and many thanks for
your excellent navigation and steadying
influence on the rest of us, when things
went "hay wire" and thanks for sticking
with me over Belgium on Dec 6th 1944
that is something I shall never forget
you for.

All best wishes for the future
and keep in touch.

Yours ever,

George (Stew Lee).

P.T.O.

162, Boothroyd Lane,
Dewsbury.
21st Dec. 1955.

Dear Don,

Many thanks for your card, letter
and "ticking off". I am sorry that I have
not written before, but things have been
rather hectic. Anne has been suffering from
a slipped disc since August, and is just
getting about now, so I have been rather
busy one way and another.

Talking about laying an egg, I also
remember another time, when there were only
two members of a certain crew left aboard,
and I am not quite sure who laid the
most eggs. There we were, 14,000', nothing on
the clock except the makers name, no power,
just four blades revolving 'round and 'round,
that were neither use nor ornament, talk
about "Gremlins", they worked overtime that night.
I think you and I must have had some

very good friends among the 'Gremi' who used "sky hooks" to carry the 'crate' across the channel.

Enough of past glories, frights and that have you. I sincerely hope that you and your family are all keeping well, and looking forward to the "festive season".

I will now bring this amazing epistle to a close by wishing you and yours a very Merry Christmas and a Happy New Year from all here.

Yours
With best wishes,
George . 'I'

Extracts from 'A Tribute to George Lee' by his son, David

George Lee was born in November 1914, just three months after the start of the First World War – the war that was to change society for ever and was to sow the seeds of the Second World War, in which he was to play a part. This part was for the many thousands like him, a small but consuming influence on their lives, which was the case with my father until his death in November 1973.

He volunteered to join the National Fire Service in Dewsbury, and as the war progressed he felt that he should undertake a greater involvement in the war effort. In August 1942 he enlisted in the Royal Air Force and qualified as a pilot. In October 1944 he began flying on operations in the Lancaster bomber with 166 Squadron.

George Lee was not a national hero, unknown to the world at large during that time, but like many thousands of young men and women who had to serve their country, he was in the last analysis a small part of a great machine. He and his crew together did what they considered to be their duty, in order to save their country from domination by an alien regime. While there is much talk and research into the effects of war on the innocent victims of war, my father was also an innocent victim of war. He, like the many others, both military and civilian, were thrown into that war by the mistakes of an earlier age, and the folly of old men. The stress and fear that he encountered during the years spent fighting in the war took its toll, ageing him beyond his years. He was unable to forget the horrors that he had seen, perhaps unwilling to accept what he had taken part in, the death and destruction brought by the bombing campaign against Germany. He said of this – 'If they (the aircrew) had stopped to think of what they were doing, then they could not have done it'.

On a personal note I believe that what these young men witnessed from above was too shocking to take in, and it is perhaps one reason why their recoil from this terror was in the form of heavy drinking, which took place after the raids that they had taken part in. That is not meant as criticism, but more of a realisation of the effects of untold stress that they encountered. These men were not fanatics, or warmongers, only young men thrown into a war that they had not created, nor did they want that war. It is the politicians who create the situations that lead to war, but it is civilians who suffer the consequences of the effects of any war. Of course, we look for enemies in time of war, but 'it is war itself that is the true enemy'.

David Lee, December 2005

Glossary

Cookie: Extremely long 4,000lb cylindrical bomb, already primed for detonation on impact.

Feathering: On engine failure, a method of turning the propeller blades edge-on to the airflow to prevent them from causing drag while 'windmilling'.

Gee: A navigation aid consisting of identifying radar pulses with phased intervals, sent from stations in England, which were displayed on a cathode ray tube in the navigator's compartment, enabling the navigator to lock any two pulses on the screen and obtain the aircraft's position.

H2S: From a large bowl beneath the aircraft, radar pulses were transmitted downwards, rotating by means of an internal aerial. On hitting the ground the pulses were reflected back to the aerial and fed into a receiver which transferred them onto a cathode ray screen in the navigator's compartment. A scanning line from the centre of the screen rotated with the aerial movement and when the pulses reflected from a built-up area or a coastline, they left blobs on the screen which retained them while a pattern was built up of the territory below, enabling the navigator to identify his position.

Pathfinder Systems:
(a) Oboe:
A radar system which made accurate location of the target by means of beams sent from land stations to the aircraft which returned them, allowing the ground station to measure the aircraft position and to allow another station to send out beams to a cathode ray tube in the aircraft showing dots on one side of the beam and dashes on the other to ensure the aircraft maintained the correct course and distance to the target.

171

(b) Systems for marking targets:

(1) Newhaven: Ground marking of target by visual means.

(2) Paramatta: Ground marking by use of radar.

(3) Wanganui: Sky marking of bomb-release point to hit the target using radar – Oboe or H2S.

(4) Sky markers: Parachute flares of various colours released by means of Oboe (usually) when dense cloud prevented use of ground target indicators.

(5) Target indicators: Flares with barometric fuses to ignite at low level and send a cascade of fire onto the ground which would burn for several minutes in various pre-set colours.

(6) Window: Bundles of metallized strips of paper pushed from a small chute in the aircraft to jam enemy radar searching for the bomber stream.

(7) German dummy targets: Dummy targets were set up in fields near to towns, with anti-aircraft guns, searchlights and coloured target indicators to entice pilots to think they were attacking the real target.

(8) Pathfinder Force: It was the technical brilliance and the bravery of the Pathfinder Force which enabled bomber crews to find and destroy German targets, thereby bringing the European War to a successful conclusion.

Index